Lost Horizon Companion

D1523253

Lost Horizon Companion

*A Guide to the James Hilton Novel
and Its Characters, Critical
Reception, Film Adaptations and
Place in Popular Culture*

JOHN R. HAMMOND

McFarland & Company, Inc., Publishers
Jefferson, North Carolina, and London

LIBRARY OF CONGRESS CATALOGUING-IN-PUBLICATION DATA

Hammond, J. R. (John R.), 1933–
    Lost Horizon companion : a guide to the James Hilton
  novel and its characters, critical reception, film adaptations
  and place in popular culture / by John R. Hammond.
        p.   cm.
    Includes bibliographical references and index.

    ISBN-13: 978-0-7864-3238-7
    softcover : 50# alkaline paper ∞

    1. Hilton, James, 1900–1954. Lost Horizon — Handbooks,
  manuals, etc.   2. Hilton, James, 1900–1954 — Film and video
  adaptations.   3. Hilton, James, 1900–1954 — Influence.   I. Title.
  PR6015.I53L64   2008
  823'.912 — dc22   2007044744

British Library cataloguing data are available

Cover illustration: Peak in the Kuen Lun Range, drawn by Major
Strutt from a sketch by Robert Shaw, 1871

Manufactured in the United States of America

McFarland & Company, Inc., Publishers
  Box 611, Jefferson, North Carolina 28640
  www.mcfarlandpub.com

Table of Contents

Acknowledgments

This book would have been much the poorer but for the help received from many quarters. I owe a considerable debt of thanks to my friend Kurt Kausler, Hiltonian collector and aficionado. He has been indefatigable in locating elusive book reviews, articles and newspaper cuttings; my task would have been immeasurably more difficult without his help. My colleagues in the James Hilton Society, especially Laurence Price and Keith Minton, have been enormously helpful and encouraging.

I should also thank R. Dixon Smith of Cambridge, England, who has kindly provided me with stills from the classic film version of *Lost Horizon* and given me much helpful advice.

The Archivist of Macmillan Publishers Ltd., Alysoun Sanders, has been most helpful to me in my researches and I wish to express my warm thanks to her.

I would like to thank the staffs of the following libraries for their assistance: National Newspaper Library, Colindale; Bodleian Library, Oxford; Nottingham Trent University.

My final debt is to my wife, Jean, who has been unfailingly patient and forbearing throughout the travails of writing and researching this book.

John Hammond

Preface

There can be few novelists who can claim to have added a word to the English language and also created a much loved fictional character. Both statements can be applied to the British novelist and script writer James Hilton, who coined the name "Shangri-La" in *Lost Horizon*, first published in 1933, and in his story *Goodbye Mr. Chips* created an affectionate portrait of a revered schoolmaster, "Chips," whose name has become synonymous with gentleness and wisdom.

The term "Shangri-La" is now widely known and is applied to any peaceful idyll or retreat from the world. The word has found a place in numerous dictionaries and encyclopedias and is known and understood even by those who may not have read Hilton's novel. A.C. Ward in the *Longman Companion to Twentieth Century Literature* (London: Longman, 1975) states, "The term has since been used of any such supposed place of withdrawal from the distresses of ordinary life, a lotus land," and William Rose Benet in *The Reader's Encyclopedia* (New York: Crowell, 1965) states, "Shangri-La has come to mean any ideal refuge."

In addition to writing *Lost Horizon* and *Goodbye Mr. Chips* James Hilton wrote other best selling novels including *Random Harvest* (1941) and *So Well Remembered* (1945), but today his reputation rests primarily on *Lost Horizon*, which has been continuously in print on both sides of the Atlantic since 1933. It has been filmed (twice), dramatized for radio on numerous occasions and even adapted as a stage musical. The novel is unusual in that it has attracted both popular and critical acclaim. Always popular with the reading public, *Lost Horizon* is available in a variety of mass market paperback editions and shows no sign of losing its appeal.

1

Also respected by the academic community, *Lost Horizon* won the Hawthornden Prize in 1934 (the British equivalent of the Pulitzer) and continues to be studied in universities as part of courses on fantasy.

The present companion aims to offer an introduction to the novel which will be of service to the student and the general reader. The opening chapter provides a summary of Hilton's life and times and describes his circumstances at the time of writing the novel. This is followed by three chapters providing a summary of the plot of the novel, a glossary of words and phrases which may require explication to a 21st century reader, and an alphabetically arranged guide to the novel's characters.

The chapter entitled "Reception" looks at critical and popular reception of the book and focuses in particular on the reviews which appraised the story from literary, imaginative and utopian standpoints.

Chapter 6, "Texts," looks at the publishing history of the novel and the various editions which are now available.

Chapter 7, "Contexts," examines the social, cultural and international context surrounding the publication of *Lost Horizon* in 1933 including the exploration of Tibet, the growth of air travel, the rise of Hitler to power and the gathering war clouds. Chapter 8, "Narrative Art," looks at Hilton's style and use of language, his literary techniques and the skilful manner in which the personality of the leading character, Conway, is gradually unfolded.

Chapter 9, "Ideas," examines the issues and themes discussed in the novel, its philosophical basis and its place in the history of utopian fiction.

Chapter 10, "Film Versions and Other Adaptations," discusses the movie adaptations of *Lost Horizon*, focusing in particular on the 1937 version directed by Frank Capra, which is now regarded as a milestone in the history of film. Chapter 11, "*Lost Horizon* and the Modern World," looks at responses to the novel over the past 70 years including academic criticism of the book and the various sequels by other writers. Why has *Lost Horizon* always been so popular when so many novels published in the 1930s have faded into oblivion? This is followed by some recommended Questions for Discussion (Appendix 1), which students and reading groups may find helpful. The Appendices also include Hilton's own preface to *Lost Horizon*, brief biographies of Hilton's friends, and a *Lost Horizon* chronology.

I hope that this volume will be found of value both as an introduction to the novel and as a stimulus to further reading and discussion. In his study, *Critical Approaches to Literature* (Englewood Cliffs, N.J.: Prentice-Hall, 1956), David Daiches observed that literary criticism is "not an end in itself, but a means to the greater understanding and appreciation of literary works." If this guide encourages more readers to return to *Lost Horizon* and to follow it with heightened insight and enjoyment, my end will have been served.

A Note About Editions

Page references to the text of *Lost Horizon* are to the Pocket Books edition of the novel (New York: Simon & Schuster, frequently reprinted). Quotations from *Lost Horizon* are cited parenthetically within the text.

1

The Author

In the spring of 1933 an unknown young man named James Hilton submitted the manuscript of a novel entitled *Blue Moon* to the reputable and long established London publisher Macmillan. The publisher sought the opinion of their reader, the writer and critic J.C. Squire (later Sir John Squire), who reported favorably upon it, strongly recommending acceptance. At the time neither the author nor the publisher could have had any inkling that this novel, later to be known under the title *Lost Horizon*, was to become a runaway bestseller and was to add a new word to the English language: Shangri-La.

Let us take a closer look at this unknown young man.

Beginnings

James Hilton was born on September 9, 1900, at 26 Wilkinson Street, Leigh, Lancashire, the only son of John Hilton and his wife, Elizabeth. John and Elizabeth had married in 1898, when John was twenty-six and Elizabeth (formerly Burch) was twenty-eight. Both had been schoolteachers, John having been on the staff of Forest Road School, Walthamstow, a suburb of London, at the time of their wedding. Although both were living in Walthamstow in 1900 they wanted their baby to be born in their home town of Leigh and in the house of John's grandfather.

Leigh, situated five miles from Wigan and sixteen miles from Manchester, was then a thriving manufacturing town, based on cotton, engineering and coal mining. At that time it had a population of 40,000. Wilkinson Street consists of a long terrace of Victorian houses with small front gardens and bay windows: the kind of houses which appealed to the young professionals of the time. James's parents only remained in Leigh for a short period, soon returning to Walthamstow, yet they must have returned to Leigh from time to time to visit family and friends for James retained many memories of his Lancashire roots. In later years Leigh became the background for two of his novels, *And Now Goodbye* and *So Well Remembered*, and for at least two short stories, "Gerald and the Candidate" and "My Aunt Lavinia."

John Hilton was an important influence on James with his love of classical music and his belief in the value of a sound education. In later years music was to appear as a motif in many of James's novels.

In October 1906 James was admitted as a pupil at Maynard Road School, Walthamstow, within walking distance of his home at 16 College Road. He wrote later, "At the age of six, my mother led me through suburban streets for presentation to the headmistress at the nearest Infants Department."[1]

He was a bright pupil, for he came from a home which encouraged education and was surrounded by books including the works of Dickens, Thackeray and Jules Verne.

He remained at the elementary school until 1911, when he was enrolled at the George Monoux School, Walthamstow, a grammar school which had been established in 1527. Here he received a good foundation in Latin grammar and also learned French, German and Greek. His favorite subjects were English literature, history and music.

When world war began in August 1914 James was almost 14 and had already won a scholarship to a public school in Hertfordshire, Haileybury College. He did not commence his studies there as his father, a staunch pacifist, had discovered that the school possessed a rifle range and an Officers' Training Corps and strongly disapproved of these. James remained at home for a time, busying himself by learning Russian and applying for posts in London — including a post at a Russian bank for which he was almost successful. He wrote later:

My father, however, was beginning to dally again with the idea of a public-school for me, and soon conceived the idea that since he could not make up his mind, I should choose a school for myself. So I toured England on this eccentric but interesting quest.[2]

He traveled the length and breadth of England by train, visiting schools in York, Cheltenham, Brighton, Sherborne and elsewhere, interviewing headmasters and inspecting schools. Even today this would be considered decidedly unusual, and at that time it must have seemed revolutionary. At last he made his decision: "Eventually, I spent a weekend at Cambridge and liked the town and university atmosphere so much that I finally made the choice, despite the fact that the school there possessed both the rifle-range and the cadet corps."[3]

He did not tell his father about the latter and enrolled at The Leys School midway through the summer term of 1915, remaining there until 1918. He was happy at The Leys; he never received corporal punishment, nor was he bullied, nor became involved in fights with other pupils. The only times he transgressed against school rules were when he left the campus to enjoy a lazy afternoon at the Orchard, Grantchester (a tea garden formerly patronized by Rupert Brooke), or to attend evensong at King's College Chapel. While at The Leys he became editor of the school magazine, *The Leys Fortnightly*, and was a prolific contributor of short stories, poems and articles. One of them, "Lucifer," is a lively and evocative piece about a Zeppelin shot down in flames over the Hertfordshire hills. Another, "The Bayonet," is an astute piece on the folly of war. He also wrote a striking short story in the manner of Chekhov, "Ignis Fatuus," which tells the story of a simple and illiterate Russian peasant who fights in the world war, becomes involved in the Revolution and then decides to return home, searching in vain for his native village. When the *Lusitania* was sunk in May 1915 James wrote a poem about it which was published in the *Cambridge Magazine*, a pacifist weekly, edited by C.K. Ogden, who later invented Basic English.

During his years at The Leys James made one of the decisive encounters of his life, Mr. W.H. Balgarnie, known affectionately to generations of Leysians as "Uncle." Balgarnie was senior classics master at the school for many years and was a member of the staff from 1900 to 1929 and again from 1940 to 1946. Balgarnie became a Leysian institution, taking a keen and benevolent interest in all aspects of the school, entertaining pupils for tea at his home, editing the school directory, supervising games, reminiscing about the past and making Latin jokes. When later James described Mr. Chips as "the guest of honor at Old Brookfeldian dinners, the court of appeal in all matters affecting Brookfield history and traditions,"[4] he undoubtedly had in mind Balgarnie as a large part of his inspiration. Kindly yet firm, avuncular yet shrewd, he made a deep impression on Hilton: an impression that remained with him throughout life. After Balgarnie's death in 1951 at the age of 82, Hilton wrote to the then headmaster of The Leys, Dr. Humphrey, saying, "Balgarnie was, I suppose, the chief model for my story, so far as I had one; certainly in my school life his was a personality I have never forgotten."[5]

One delightful anecdote about Hilton and Balgarnie is worth recording. The classics master had set an essay on a topical subject of the day, and James duly submitted his contribution. That evening James was summoned to Balgarnie's study. "Hilton," he said, "you would have done better to alter a few of the words and phrases in the essay you sent in instead of copying verbatim from the article in *The Times*. Schoolmasters do read, you know." "Well, Sir," replied Hilton, "as the subject matter was just what was required, I thought the article I had contributed to *The Times* would also do for the essay."[6]

Meanwhile the war was having an increasing impact on school life. Each Sunday after chapel lists of casualties were read out; bayonet practice was held on the football field; playing fields were ploughed up for trenches and drill grounds. It was impossible to overlook the war since it invaded all aspects of the school. The cadet corps was now of growing importance, although James declined the invitation to join since he disliked regimentation. "Slowly, inch by inch," he wrote, "the tide of war lapped to the gates of our seclusion.... [O]ffenders gated for cigarette smoking in January were dropping bombs from the sky in December."[7] James belonged to a generation which was just too young to serve in the war, although those only a little older than himself were being conscripted. This daily awareness of death, added to the knowledge that he could be called up for military service at any time, formed the background to his life throughout those tumultuous years. When the war came to an end in November 1918 he was in uniform waiting for a summons which never came. It must have seemed a last-minute reprieve, and he felt it was a miracle that he was still alive.

His years at The Leys were of crucial importance to his literary development. He was reading widely, including such seminal works as Arnold Bennett's *Clayhanger*, H.G. Wells's *The New Machiavelli* and Bernard Shaw's *Major Barbara*. He was contributing regularly to the school magazine, including short stories and essays, gaining valuable experience in the writing of fiction and the shaping of narrative. Most significantly of all he began work on a novel — later published under the title *Catherine Herself*— commencing the first draft in the Sixth Form Prep Room, (now the Moulton Room) at the precocious age of 17.

From the autumn of 1918 to the summer of 1921 James was an undergraduate at Christ's College, Cambridge, completing his studies in 1921 with a B.A. (a Bachelor of Arts degree) in History and English. He then spent a further year at Christ's as a Research Scholar. There can be no doubt that he was happy at Cambridge and regarded it with great affection. Cambridge figures prominently in several of his novels including most notably *Random Harvest*— where the central character, Charles Rainer, is a Cambridge student — and *Time and Time Again*, whose hero Charles Anderson "loved Cambridge with an ache."[8] Both these novels should be studied carefully for their insight into James's thoughts and feelings during these years. For him and his student contemporaries the town and the university were indelibly

James Hilton at the outset of his literary career, circa 1920 (courtesy the James Hilton Society).

9

associated with the unique atmosphere of that time, one in which the war with its daily catalogue of slaughter was the dominant background.

In 1920, while he was still an undergraduate, *Catherine Herself* was published. It had been accepted by the reputable publisher Fisher Unwin in their "First Novel Library." *Catherine Herself* belongs to a literary genre which academics call a Bildungsroman — that is to say, a novel of adolescence, or a novel of development, which traces the history of the hero or heroine from childhood to maturity. In this case the central character is Catherine Weston, a strong-willed young woman who is consumed with an ambition to be a successful concert pianist. The novel traces the story of her childhood and adolescence, her emotional experiences, and her gradual coming to terms with her own limitations. The story ends with Catherine accepting the fact that she will never be a famous virtuoso, and acknowledging that she has made many mistakes because of her own naïveté, and selfishness. Though the novel is immature and at times over-written it remains a remarkable piece of work for a twenty-year-old author.

The most interesting parts of the book are the descriptions of the area around Walthamstow, Woodford Green and Epping Forest (an area which James knew and remembered well from his boyhood years) and the portrait of Catherine's father, John Weston, which must surely reflect facets of James's father, John Hilton. It is also characteristic of Hilton's novels that there are many reflections about music, literature and culture.

On its publication *Catherine Herself* was favorably reviewed. *The Nation*, for example, stated: "The vigor of the character drawing, the directness of observation shown by Mr. Hilton prove him to be a born novelist." In their review *Bookman* praised the novel warmly, stating: "The whole is original, suggestive, and full of intuitive perception.... This is a novel that holds the attention because it is a good story as well as a very interesting essay in the psychology of suggestion." The *Evening Standard* also praised the book, adding: "Catherine seems to be a creation of whom many a more mature novelist might be proud."[9]

It is interesting to note that though Hilton tended to disown his early novels once he had achieved commercial success he did not disown *Catherine Herself,* for it appeared at the top of his list of works for many years, and was still heading the list as late as 1947. Macmillan also reissued *Catherine Herself* in 1934 as part of a uniform edition of his novels.

In 1921 James's parents, John and Elizabeth Hilton, moved to a house at Oak Hill Gardens, Woodford Green, Essex, a pleasant area situated close to Epping Forest. The Forest, opened by Queen Victoria in 1882, is an extensive public park wooded with fine beech trees.

On leaving Cambridge James joined his parents at Oak Hill Gardens and spent the next ten years and more living quietly with them, earning his "bread and butter" by writing a twice-weekly column for an Irish newspaper, the *Dublin Independent*, and by contributing book reviews to the *Daily Telegraph*, the *Manchester Guardian*, the *Daily News* and the *Star*. In his spare time he toiled away at a series of novels, none of which achieved commercial success. He commented later: "I read twenty novels a week, reviewing eight out of the lot, wrote two special articles, and put in a few hours at night on a novel."[10]

When he was not working he would go for long walks or cycle rides, play the piano (at which he excelled) and travel in continental Europe.

Throughout these years he was gaining useful experience in the art of writing. Although none of his full-length fiction brought him fame and fortune it was the apprenticeship through which a tyro taught himself the art of the novelist. His early novels, *Storm Passage* (1922), *The Passionate Year* (1923), *The Dawn of Reckoning* (1925) and *The Meadows of the Moon* (1926), are little read today and arguably do not fulfill the promise shown by his first novel, *Catherine Herself*. They are rather melodramatic in content, consisting largely of conversation spoken by characters who are not fully convincing as flesh-and-blood men and women. They are introspective novels, interesting as studies of human nature yet lacking those literary qualities which make a novel stand out from the crowd. In later years when he had become an established literary figure his publishers sought his permission to reprint these early novels, most of which were out of print. Hilton resisted this, feeling that "some of the work was not of a sufficiently high standard, and he did not want to let his public down."[11]

In the 1920s he was still a young man learning his craft, and lacked that experience of life which is so essential to the writing of a successful novel. It was not until the publication of *Terry* in 1927 that for the first time he achieved a full-length work of fiction with solid, believable characters who live and breathe. *Terry* stands out among his early work as a wholly convincing narrative possessing the craftsmanship and sweep of a major novel. It is also unusual in that Hilton himself is a character in the story.

Terry tells the story of a research scientist who is shy and aloof but is at the same time sensitive and compassionate. He feels guilty following his affair with Helen Severn, the wife of a prominent politician, and decides to leave England and work in Vienna as an assistant to an unscrupulous scientist, Karelsky. How he works out his own salvation, comes to terms with his shyness and eventually finds lasting happiness is told with realism and skill.

Terry himself—whose real name is Terrington—the politician Geoffrey Severn; his wife, Helen; his daughter June; and Mizzi, the hotel owner, are drawn with total conviction in a narrative which seems to flow seamlessly. In this sense the novel is a marked advance on the melodramatic plots of *The Passionate Year* and *Storm Passage* for, while it certainly possesses moments of high drama, there is nothing that jars on the reader's credulity. The device of the author becoming a character himself is a clever touch and works well. At one point Hilton is told "The fact is, you're born, in my opinion, to be a successful novel writer. You've just got the right mixture of brains, sentiment, and conventionality."[12]

Most remarkable of all is the fact that *Terry* contains an interesting anticipation of the central theme of *Lost Horizon*. The narrator comments:

> I am thinking, of course, of the great Tibetan monastery sensation.
> Karelsky traveled, apparently in Tibet, and somehow or other
> obtained an entrance into an old and inaccessible monastery in
> which, to his astonishment, he found that his own methods of
> rejuvenation had been practiced for hundreds of years; so that, in
> fact, many of the monks were actually in their third and fourth
> centuries.[13]

This anticipation of the central plot device of his most celebrated novel six years prior to its publication is indeed striking. (Later Hilton was to rework the main theme of *Terry* in his novel *Nothing So Strange* [1948]— in fact *Nothing So Strange* could be described as "the Americanization of

Terry"). It is regrettable that *Terry* is so little known today, for it surely merits republication as one of the most promising and well written of Hilton's works.

Terry was followed by *The Silver Flame*, published in 1928. *The Silver Flame* can be regarded as the last of his apprentice novels, for by now he was approaching literary success. This novel spans the years 1897–1926 and tells the story of a spirited heroine, Margaret Frensham, and her life and loves. She experiences different kinds of love and eventually has to choose between the ardent admiration of a younger man and the steadfast devotion of a more mature figure. She opts for the latter and in looking back on her life at the age of fifty reflects that:

> All the mystery of heaven and earth lay in that process of being young, of growing older, of being old. To her, at the middle stage, the past and the future balanced perfectly in her heart. She would be quite happy. The flame of love, that had been so golden at noonday, would turn to silver in the evening.[14]

Summarized in these terms *The Silver Flame* sounds rather trite, yet it is one of the most thoughtful and substantial of his early works. The characterization is accomplished and the story line is carried forward with skill. As a panorama of English life during the first quarter of the twentieth century the novel is of absorbing interest, with world events being interwoven in the narrative against a background of English scenery and manners.

Hilton himself seems to have thought highly of it, for this and *Catherine Herself* were the only ones of his early titles he would permit to be reprinted. As late as 1937 Macmillan was reprinting it in a cheap edition and even later, in 1949, it was reissued in the United States in an abridged version under the title *Three Loves Had Margaret*.

Being a freelance journalist is a precarious business at the best of times but in the 1920s it was especially so. Thousands of young men had returned from the war in search of employment and Hilton was therefore trying to launch his career at a difficult time. Looking back on Hilton's literary career in the 1920s one cannot but admire his dogged determination to be a writer — indeed, he does not seem to have seriously considered any other vocation. From the moment when he started work on *Catherine Herself* to the publication of his first successful novels in the 1930s he pursued with relentless earnestness his determination to be a novelist. Despite disappointing sales — he confessed later that "the average sales of my novels could usually be counted on the legs of a dozen centipedes"[15] — he did not give up but persevered with novel after novel in the conviction that one day he would achieve success.

Throughout these years he was honing his distinctive style and perfecting the art of narrative. He was deeply influenced by Somerset Maugham, Maurice Baring and Edith Wharton, favoring an economical style of writing devoid of "floweriness" and pretension. His preferred method of composition was to type out a rough first draft, often typing at great speed to set down his first thoughts, and then go over the manuscript with care, marking corrections and additions in ink. Working in this manner he produced no fewer than seven novels between 1920 and 1930, a remarkable achievement when one reflects that the writing of fiction had to be done in his "spare" time when he was not working on book reviews or articles.

In 1931 came the first of his novels to achieve commercial success, *And Now Goodbye*, which he described as "the first novel I wrote which I really liked."[16] The idea for the story came to him one day when he happened to read a newspaper report of a clergyman in an industrial town who had run away with a young woman, a member of his own congregation. Expressed thus baldly the clergyman's behavior sounded reprehensible, but Hilton asked himself the questions: Were there no redeeming features? Was it really as sordid as it appeared?

And Now Goodbye is set in a northern industrial town named "Browdley," a fictional version of Hilton's home town of Leigh in Lancashire. The central character, Howat Freemantle, is a clergyman married to an invalid wife and caught up in the humdrum routine of a minister. The opening chapters give a vivid impression of his life and background, his struggle to keep his congregation together, to manage the church finances, and to maintain harmony in his household. He meets an attractive young woman, Elizabeth Garland, who comes to him for German lessons, but after having known her for a few weeks he learns she has left her home and run away. Rumors begin to circulate that she has eloped with a married man, bringing disgrace to her parents. Her mother and father, pillars of the church, are horrified at her behavior and disown her.

Freemantle has arranged to visit London on some church business but before embarking on his journey receives a letter from Elizabeth Garland asking him to assure her parents that she is safe and well. He asks her to meet him in London so that he can plead with her to return home. When he meets her he learns that the rumors are false and that she is simply planning to travel to Vienna to learn to play the violin. She will be traveling alone: there is no "married man" at all. Greatly relieved at this news, Freemantle dines with the girl and the two go to a concert together, for they discover a mutual love of classical music. They spend the evening together and become deeply attracted to one another. He tells her of his loneliness, his discontent with his life in Browdley, his unfulfilled ambitions and the solace he finds in music and literature. She in turn tells him she had wanted to know him better but in the past had failed to penetrate his barrier of shyness. Eventually they declare their love for one another and resolve to travel to Vienna together: he is so deeply attracted to her that he has decided to leave his wife and abandon his work as a clergyman. The novel ends tragically, when the train on which they are both traveling crashes; Freemantle survives but Elizabeth receives fatal injuries.

And Now Goodbye was widely and favorably reviewed. The New York *Herald Tribune* praised the book, describing it as "a fine novel, for those who appreciate skill in writing and observation coupled with human sympathy and tenderness." The *New York Times Book Review* described the novel as "Beautifully written, deftly constructed, tense, dramatic and with a leading character who lingers in one's memory, *And Now Goodbye* is a genuine work of art ... a novel of high quality." The *Baltimore Evening Sun* concluded, "Mr. Hilton's style is tinctured with humor and irony ... an unusual novel, to be read and savored, as well for its manner and its matter."[17] Hilton must have been well satisfied with its favorable reception and with the fact that for the first time he was earning respectable royalties. In 1937 the novel was dramatized as a play by Philip Howard and in 1940 it was adapted as a film screenplay by Hilton himself, but a film version did not materialize.

His next three novels, *Murder at School* (1931), *Contango* (1932) and *Knight without Armor* (1933), are all interesting experiments. *Murder at School* is a detective story on the familiar pattern of Agatha Christie and Dorothy L. Sayers (Hilton had been advised that a detective story was certain to be a lucrative proposition) with a young sleuth, Colin Revell, attempting to unravel a murder mystery at his old school, Oakington. The story is ingeniously worked out and is now regarded as a classic of its kind. Under its alternative title *Was It Murder?* it was reprinted by Oxford University Press in 1989 in their "Classic Crime" series. It is still in print today, by the British publisher Swallowtail.

At first sight *Contango* (published in the U.S. under the title *Ill Wind*) appears to be a series of loosely connected short stories but it is actually a novel illustrating how apparently unrelated events can impinge on one another. Ranging in setting from Switzerland to New York and from South America to California it demonstrates the unpredictable manner in which random occurrences and actions can have completely unforeseen consequences on others. The novel is further evidence of Hilton's ability to make use of widely differing backgrounds and to be equally at home among businessmen, film stars, inventors and hoteliers. Once again the book received favorable reviews. The New York *Herald Tribune* described it as "a moving and extraordinary book ... the promise of great things to come," while in Britain the *Manchester Guardian* hailed it as a "really triumphant success.... No intelligent reader should miss the book."[18] *Knight without Armor* (published in the U.S. under the title *Without Armor*) is a fast moving adventure story set in Russia during the Revolution. It tells the story of an Englishman who travels to Russia as a teacher and journalist and is unwittingly caught up in the Revolution and the civil war. After many exciting adventures, during which he tries to save the life of an aristocrat, he returns to Britain and dies without anyone appreciating his extraordinary story. The novel reveals Hilton's insight into Russian life and his gift for communicating the atmosphere of war and revolution, even though he had not in fact visited that country. One of the underlying purposes of the story is to illustrate the depravity and cruelty of which human beings are capable yet at the same time reveal the nobility and compassion of the human spirit. Hilton wrote in the

Preface that he felt "that Russia during the first quarter of the century was probably the biggest anvil on which world history was being hammered out; and therefore, ipso facto, it must be grand territory for the novelist."[19] He admitted to a personal fondness for the book and said he had enjoyed writing it. It was later filmed starring Robert Donat and Marlene Dietrich. The film was the brainchild of the impresario Alexander Korda and was highly praised by the critics.

Success at Last

During the winter of 1932–1933 he began work on the research for the novel which eventually became *Lost Horizon*. He spent many hours in the British Library absorbing accounts of Tibetan history and topography, soaking himself in the writings of explorers, geographers and adventurers. The actual writing of the book took him six weeks during March and April 1933, working at his home at Woodford Green. When it was completed he submitted it to Macmillan, a distinguished publishing house established in 1843. This was a bold move on Hilton's part; most of his earlier novels had been published by Thornton Butterworth or by Ernest Benn, but he clearly felt he would like to be regarded as a Macmillan author. When he learned that the novel had been accepted he began to have second thoughts about its title. On 9 May 1933 he wrote to the publishers expressing his doubts:

> Dear Mr. Macmillan,
> I have for some time been feeling that *Blue Moon* is not a particularly good title for the new book, especially as so many people seem to think it has a musical comedy flavor. This morning my American publisher has cabled me to the same effect and says also that the title has been used already in the U.S.
> I think, apart from getting a better title, it would be an advantage to have the same one on both sides, and I hope, if you agree, to have an alternative suggestion ready in a day or two.

Two days later he was able to write again with his preferred title: "I am glad you are in agreement that *Blue Moon* could be improved upon, and I believe Mr. Squire thought so too. My own preference for an alternative is *Lost Horizon*, which seems to me both appropriate and attractive."[20]

Macmillan published *Lost Horizon* on 26 September 1933 in an edition of 3,000 copies, with a further 3,000 printed in November. As the novel is now known throughout the world and has been consistently in print since 1933 it is easy to jump to the conclusion that it was an immediate best seller, but this was not in fact the case. At first sales were slow, to Hilton's acute disappointment. He had had high expectations that the book would sell widely and was disheartened when this did not happen. In any event sales did not take off until 1934, and this was due to

The Hilton family home at Oak Hill Gardens, Woodford Green, Essex, where *Lost Horizon* was written. Formerly called "Leigh," the house has since been renamed "Shangri-La" (courtesy Adrienne Reynolds).

[NUMBER 207]

A page from the original manuscript of *Lost Horizon* (courtesy Curtis Brown Group).

two factors, both of which occurred in June of that year: the award of the Hawthornden Prize and the publication of *Goodbye Mr. Chips*.

The Hawthornden Prize, inaugurated in 1919, was a prize awarded annually for the best piece of imaginative writing published during the preceding year by a British author under forty-one years of age.... The organizers stated in their publicity that "originality of treatment, style, and matter are all taken into consideration." The judges included Sir John Squire and Robert Lynd, and the prize was an award of £100; a considerable sum of money in 1934 (the average weekly wage in Britain at that time was between £2 and £3). To have been awarded the Hawthornden Prize at the age of 33 was a considerable achievement for Hilton. The presentation ceremony, held in London on 14 June 1934 and attended by a distinguished gathering of writers, critics and publishers, inevitably generated useful publicity and brought his name before a wider audience. There is also the point that Sir John Squire and Robert Lynd were valuable contacts for Hilton to have made. Squire was the editor of the *London Mercury*, an important literary monthly, and had formerly been literary editor of the *New Statesman*. He was a highly influential journalist, essayist and critic. Robert Lynd was also a well known journalist who wrote under the pseudonym "Y.Y." and was a frequent contributor to the *Daily News* and the *New Statesman*. In being awarded the prize Hilton was in good company, for previous prizewinners had included Charles Morgan's *The Fountain* (1932) and Siegfried Sassoon's *Memoirs of a Fox Hunting Man* (1928).

In the autumn of 1933 Hilton was invited to write a 3,000 word short story for the Christmas supplement of the *British Weekly*, an influential and long established publication. He would be paid 30 guineas for this — a respectable sum of money in 1933 — but the snag was it had to be written and submitted to the editor within two weeks. That was the deadline. He recalled later:

> A whole week out of my precious two was spent in a blue funk, thinking I just could not go on with the job. I had no ideas, no plot, no anything.
> Then, one foggy winter morning I got out my bicycle and determined to run away from my hag-ridden self. I was enjoying the

The dust jacket of the original edition of *Lost Horizon*, published by Macmillan, London, in 1933 (courtesy Pan Macmillan).

keen air and the exercise when, suddenly, an idea bobbed up and I saw my whole story in a flash. I rode back home as hard as I could go and in four days I had banged out the whole thing.

That was *Goodbye Mr. Chips*! It duly appeared and got some mildly favorable comment and I considered it a closed chapter.[21]

The book must have been written in a *white heat* of inspiration. He said: "I don't think I have ever written before so quickly, so easily, and with such certitude that I needn't think twice about a word, a sentence, or a movement in the narrative. I had been granted that curious lift of the pen which must be called '*inspiration*.'" He added: "*Goodbye Mr. Chips* was written more quickly, more easily, and with fewer subsequent alterations than anything I had ever written before, or have ever written since."[22]

The editor of the *British Weekly* was embarrassed to find that the 3,000 words they had requested had now become 18,000, but he was so impressed with the story's quality and sincerity that he decided to go ahead with publication.

Goodbye Mr. Chips was published first as a Christmas supplement in the *British Weekly*, then by the *Atlantic Monthly*, a prestigious American magazine, where it enjoyed a tremendous reception. Book publication followed in America in June 1934 and in Britain in October 1934. Its success was immediate. Its success — following hard on the heels of the award of the Hawthornden Prize for *Lost Horizon* — launched Hilton on an extraordinarily successful career as a novelist and scriptwriter. His name became a household word, especially in the United States. After years in the doldrums he had "arrived" as an author.

It would not be an exaggeration to say that this short book launched Hilton on his literary career. This gentle story, tracing with affection the life and times of a beloved schoolmaster, is one of the most perfectly written of all his books. In portraying the life and personality of Mr. Chipping, classics master at Brookfield School from 1870 to 1918 and dying in 1933 at the age of 85, he not only distilled his memories of his own schooling at The Leys but also expressed his innermost feelings about education. Chips is not simply a dry as dust pedant but is a man whose life has been transformed by an idyllically happy marriage and who seeks to impart his gentle philosophy to generations of pupils.

Though consisting of barely 18,000 words it is one of those books which remains in the imagination long after it has been read. Written in a smooth, flowing style which seems effortless but is extraordinarily difficult to imitate, it gives a rounded portrait of a schoolmaster who is both shrewd and kindly.

Because Chips is an endearing character who dresses rather shabbily and has a quirky sense of humor it is easy to caricature the book as an apology for inefficiency and sentimentality. Yet it is in some ways an *outspoken* book, arguing against examinations and league tables comparing institutions, for example, and in favor of intellectual curiosity, and independence of mind. It can also be regarded as a meditation on the theme of Englishness — which is perhaps one reason why the book became so outstandingly popular in the United States — and on the qualities which go to make up a well rounded education. Amid all the carnage and violence of the First World War, Chips himself stands for something much more enduring — tolerance, wisdom, patience, truthfulness, and the ability to see different points of view. The book is a hymn of praise for enduring virtues: tolerance, understanding, patience, eccentricity, kindness, gentleness.

Again and again in the book there is a sense of the young James Hilton looking back with nostalgia and regret on the England we have lost — or are in danger of losing. He himself described the book as "a tribute to a great profession."[23] For all these reasons it struck a chord with thousands of readers in many lands. It was soon translated into other languages and was later filmed and dramatized.

Goodbye Mr. Chips became a publishing phenomenon. In the United States it was reprinted seventeen times between June 1934 and April 1935 and received "rave" reviews. Howard Spring in the London *Evening Standard* wrote:

> Here is a triumphant proof that a little book can be a great book. Mr. Chips deserves a place in the gallery of English characters. Never have I known more beautifully rendered a man at perfect peace with life, a finer setting forth of what happy dreams may come when you are old and gray and full of sleep.

The influential American critic Alexander Woolcott praised the book in fulsome terms, saying: "A tender and gentle story as warming to the heart and nourishing to the spirit as any I can remember.... The most profoundly moving story that has passed this way for several years."[24]

The year 1934 was therefore a turning point in Hilton's career. With the success of *Goodbye Mr. Chips* his circumstances changed from comparative poverty to affluence. With his prize money and the income from royalties he was able to move to comfortable apartments at Woodford Road, Wanstead, a short distance from his parents' home at Woodford Green (the house, then named Ingoldsby, is now renamed James Hilton House.) Describing his recreations as "music, travel and dogs," he continued to write book reviews for the *Daily Telegraph* and *Manchester Guardian* and also contributed regular reviews for the *Bookman*.

Hollywood

In the autumn of 1935 Irving Thalberg of Metro-Goldwyn-Mayer invited Hilton to come to Hollywood to assist in translating his novels to the screen. He accepted the invitation with alacrity and sailed for New York in November of that year, but before doing so married his English girlfriend, Alice Helen Brown, who had been working as a secretary at the British Broadcasting Corporation. Soon after his arrival in the U.S. he commented to a friend:

> I am optimistic about the cinema. It is pioneering, without perhaps being aware of it, into channels of human behavior which are to become increasingly important in the world of the future. And I am impressed — why not? — with the power and possibilities of its influence.[25]

Irving Thalberg was known at that time as the "boy genius" of Hollywood. He came to the film capital in 1919 and soon became head of the Universal Pictures Corporation. In 1924 he became production supervisor of the then newly formed MGM and was responsible for a series of prestigious films including *Ben Hur* (1926), *The Barretts of Wimpole Street* (1934), *Mutiny on the Bounty* (1935) and *Romeo and Juliet* (1936). Together with Louis B. Mayer he built up MGM into one of the largest and most powerful studios of the 1930s. His career was cut short by his tragically early death at the age of 37 but he was instrumental in persuading Hilton to come to Hollywood and later made an important contribution to the film version of *Goodbye Mr. Chips*.

Hollywood, nominally a suburb of Los Angeles, had been regarded as the film capital of the world since 1913. It was dominated by five giant corporations: MGM, Warner Brothers, Twentieth Century–Fox, RKO and Paramount, each with their own "stars" and their own production, distribution and exhibition facilities. The MGM studios alone comprised eighteen permanent buildings and 22 standing sets on 66 acres of land. Hollywood in the 1930s employed 1,000 writers including William Faulkner, Christopher Isherwood and Scott Fitzgerald, often paying high salaries. To the young James Hilton it must have seemed a dazzling world with limitless possibilities.

These were exciting times to be working in the film industry. Howard Koch recorded later: "With all its faults and foibles, it was Hollywood's most flourishing and fertile period in its concentration of talent, its social consciousness, and its dissemination of ideas."[26]

Hilton soon came under the wing of the American screenwriter Frances Marion, ten years his senior, who had worked on the scripts of numerous distinguished films including *Stella Dallas*, *The Scarlet Letter*, *The Big House* and *The Champ* and later worked on the script of *Knight without Armor*. His routine at this time was to rise at seven, work in his apartment all morning, then walk or bathe in the afternoons. In the evenings he either worked again or socialized with friends. During his first six months in Hollywood he lost twenty pounds in weight, so the routine must have suited him.

At first it had been Hilton's intention to maintain his home in Britain and commute between London and Hollywood, and this is what he did for some time. Between December 1935 and April 1937 he crossed the Atlantic six times. Eventually, finding the California climate congenial and that he liked Hollywood, he decided to settle permanently in America.

For some years he worked as a scriptwriter at MGM, writing the dialogue for numerous films including *Camille* (1936), starring Greta Garbo

and Robert Taylor, and *Foreign Correspondent* (1940), while also acting
as an advisor on film adaptations of his own novels. In an article
published in 1937, "The Maligned Village," he recorded his impressions
of Hollywood and his excitement at working in the film capital. He found
the experience of working there enormously stimulating and was capti-
vated by the people he met, the constant encounters with new friends, the
pleasant climate and the novelty of the world of movies. As a scriptwriter
he was granted a considerable amount of independence:

> I visited the studios as often as I liked or as often as anyone wanted
> to see me there; but the authorities seemed to realize that a writer
> is used to working on his own, and though they would have given
> me an office had I wished for one, they were quite willing for me
> to work independently.[27]

Unfortunately his wife, Alice, found it much less stimulating and the
pressures of Hollywood life plus the long absences from Britain took their
toll on his marriage. He and Alice divorced in 1937 and he then promptly
married a young actress, Galina Kopineck, but this too ended in divorce.
As his divorce from Alice and his marriage to Galina took place in Mex-
ico they were deemed invalid in U.S. law, so Alice and James were in effect
always married. They reconciled and by some accounts resumed their life
as husband and wife. Hilton took up permanent residence in California
in 1940 and became a U.S. citizen in 1948.

In Hollywood he became a member of the British "colony" resident
in the United States and became firm friends with Ronald Colman and
Greer Garson, both of whom were English by birth. Both these friends
knew the area around Epping Forest and northeast London that was familiar to Hilton. Other members of the "colony" included Leslie Howard, C.
Aubrey Smith, David Niven and Basil Rathbone. When the film version
of *Goodbye Mr. Chips* was made in 1939 Hilton was delighted with the
result and wrote to Robert Donat saying:

> I feel I must write to congratulate you on a really wonderful per-
> formance. Everybody here is raving about it, and it is indeed a
> peculiar delight to an author to see a performance which, in many
> ways, brings to actuality his own private and personal dream.[28]

The film was directed by Sam Wood and scripted by R.C. Sherriff, Claudine West and Eric Maschwitz. It did full justice to the original story and Hilton went to see the film again and again.

Meanwhile he continued to write novels and short stories. *We Are Not Alone*, published in 1937, is a powerfully written story set in an English cathedral town and describes how a hard working and modest doctor is falsely accused of having murdered his wife. Told with restraint and conviction, the novel vividly conveys the atmosphere of a small town in the early years of the twentieth century and is a plea for tolerance at a time when war clouds were already gathering. A film version, starring Paul Muni in the role of the doctor, was jointly scripted by Hilton and Milton Krims. It was described by the *Monthly Film Bulletin* as "an extraordinarily moving story, beautifully told and perfectly acted."[29] *To You Mr. Chips*, which appeared in 1938, is a collection of six short stories featuring Mr. Chips, the hero of his earlier bestseller, prefaced by a long introduction, "A Chapter of Autobiography," in which Hilton looks back with affection and candor on his years at school and university. This chapter is remarkable for its detachment and for the skilful manner in which he interweaves reminiscences of school with reflections on the world scene. In one passage he gives a striking anticipation of Orwell's *Nineteen Eighty Four*:

> All over the world today the theme and accents of barbarism are being orchestrated, while the technique of mass hypnotism, as practiced by controlled press and radio, is being schooled to construct a façade of justification for any and every excess.[30]

Once again *To You Mr. Chips* is a plea for civilized values at a time when Nazism and Fascism were rampant in Europe and when freedom of thought and expression was being increasingly eroded.

Random Harvest

Hilton's next major novel was *Random Harvest*, published in 1941. When it was issued in the United States by Little, Brown it sold 100,000 copies in six weeks. MGM promptly snapped up the film rights for $50,000.

Random Harvest is a long and complex novel, which needs to be read and reread several times to do justice to it. It was published *before* the U.S. had entered the war and at a time when Hilton had been living in America for five years. This is significant for two reasons.

Hilton was thoroughly English but the fact that he had lived on the other side of the Atlantic for five years meant that he could look at England *from the outside*. *Random Harvest* is full of asides about English characteristics, English attitudes, the English temperament and the English sense of humor. From this point of view alone it is a deeply rewarding read. The date is also significant because the novel was written at a time when America had not entered the war and Britain *stood alone* against Nazi Germany. Hilton clearly felt deeply affectionate toward England and expresses his affection in the carefully wrought story depicting one man's search for a lost happiness.

The novel tells the story of Charles Rainier, a successful businessman and politician who is haunted by a tantalizing gap in his memory and an apparent fear of his own identity. As the story proceeds the missing years of his life are gradually revealed and it becomes clear that many years previously he experienced an idyllic love affair and has been searching in vain for the woman he has lost, Paula Ridgeway. During this brief idyll he was "Smithy," a shy and idealistic young man who finds deep contentment with Paula and marries her. He is just starting to make a living by writing when a car accident robs him of his memory but reawakens his memories as Rainier. For a long time he is obsessed by the awareness of something missing from his life, by tantalizing hints of a contentment he once possessed but which now eludes him.

Behind the personal story of Paula and Smithy there is, of course, the larger story of England. It is not only Paula and Smithy who are seeking their identity but England — and for England also "it may not be too late." *Random Harvest* was written at a time when Britain's position was precarious to say the least — when invasion was a very real possibility and when it was by no means certain that Nazi Germany would be defeated. The novel is a kind of compendium of English values — tolerance, fair play, humor, gentleness.

The characterization in the novel is assured and convincing. When it was first published the book reviewer in the *New York Times* said: "It is in his portrayal of Rainier that Hilton is at his best.... *Random Harvest* is, as a whole, so good a book that one forgets its minor flaws. It is Rainier who makes the tale and he is completely real and convincing."[31]

Like Conway in *Lost Horizon* and A.J. in *Knight without Armor*, Rainier is an unassuming man who possesses leadership qualities but at the same time "had kept at heart and throughout all vicissitudes the tranquil tastes of the scholar"—to use Hilton's phrase. He knows he can never be fully happy with material success alone but yearns for the peace and happiness he had known with Paula. Like all Hilton's novels it is a *thoughtful* book, full of reflections about life, about philosophy, about human nature, and—above all—about England.

It is not difficult to see why *Random Harvest* has always been popular. It tells an absorbing story, it is well written, and it is highly readable. And it contains well drawn characters—not only Rainier and Paula, but Rainier's secretary, Harrison (who emerges as a character in his own right), and Blampied, the clergyman who befriends them and encourages Smithy to write.

One of the reasons why it is such a satisfying read is that the narrative is structured upon a series of losses and findings, and that the time scheme moves between past and present. The final paragraphs bring a *resolution* to the story by neatly resolving Rainier's search for lost happiness, Paula's search for Smithy, and the search of both of them for the place where they had both known such deep happiness.

> Then he whispered something I couldn't hear; but I knew in a flash that the gap was closed, that the random years were at an end, that the past and future would join. She knew this too, for she ran into his arms calling out: "Oh, Smithy—Smithy—it may not be too late!"[32]

The film adaptation starring Ronald Colman and Greer Garson has been described as "one of the best loved and best remembered movies of all time, teaming two of MGM's most romantic stars in a superb James Hilton story."[33] Unlike the novel, which tells the story in a series of flashbacks, the film presents the narrative in chronological order. Eloquently written by Claudine West, George Froeschel and Arthur Wimperis and brilliantly directed by Mervyn LeRoy, the film succeeds admirably in distilling the essence of the novel in a moving and absorbing entertainment. Hilton was pleased with the screenplay and contributed the opening narration introducing the movie. Of the 25 films she made in a career spanning three decades Greer Garson stated that *Random Harvest* was her personal favorite. Vivacious, happy and caring, she was perfectly cast as Paula, while Ronald Colman brought dignity and sincerity to the part of Rainier. The ending, in which Paula and Smithy are reunited outside their country cottage, has become a Hollywood legend.

Mrs. Miniver

Meanwhile Hilton was increasingly active in the world of motion pictures. On top of his work as a scriptwriter he became a vice president of the Screen Writers Guild and a member of the governing board of the Academy of Motion Picture Arts and Sciences. His outstanding success in 1942 was to be awarded an Oscar for his contribution to the film version of *Mrs. Miniver,* made by MGM and starring Greer Garson and Walter Pidgeon. The character of Mrs. Miniver had been created in 1939 by the British writer Jan Struther in a series of articles in the London *Times,* later collected together in a best selling book. She was a resourceful woman who described with humor and shrewdness the tribulations of her daily life and her humdrum experiences with her architect husband and their three children. For the film version MGM asked Hilton — together with Arthur Wimperis, George Froeschel and Claudine West — to make Mrs. Miniver the central character in a movie which would not only depict her in a peacetime setting but cast her in the role of heroine and homemaker in an embattled Britain. The result was a film which became one of the most renowned movies of the Second World War, portraying with sincerity and realism the bravery and steadfastness of the British people. The fact that it was filmed in Hollywood and not in Britain (albeit with a largely British cast) has led to accusations that it did not convey a true picture of wartime conditions. In later years Greer Garson resented this charge, saying:

> The film was made with complete integrity. It was not, as I've
> heard it spoken of, a carefully concocted propaganda film. It was
> nothing like that. It was a study of an ordinary British family — an
> upper middle class family — and how ordinary, decent people
> behave under extraordinary circumstances and stress. The stress of
> a total blitz.[34]

The British prime minister Winston Churchill predicted that the film's contribution to defeating Nazi Germany would be more powerful than a fleet of battleships. *Time* described the movie as "that almost impossible feat, a war picture that photographs the inner meaning, instead of the outward realism, of World War Two."[35]

Watching the film today it *does* seem artificial in the sense that few British families in 1939 would have lived in a large house with a maid, a cook and a car. On the other hand the wartime sequences are well done: the scenes in the air raid shelter, the armada of "little ships" sailing for Dunkirk, the fighter pilots scrambling for their planes and the family huddled in the cellar during a bombing raid, all possess the ring of truth. The portrayal of village life is convincingly realized and illustrates how the once rigid class distinctions were being eroded by the war. The film was directed by William Wyler, a perfectionist notorious for his insistence on take after take before he was satisfied.

During the years of the Second World War Hilton was at the height of his fame. The film versions of *Goodbye Mr. Chips, Mrs. Miniver* and *Random Harvest* kept his name before the public, while his novels continued to sell in enormous quantities. He was much in demand as a radio personality and could command a fee of $1750 for a guest appearance on radio programs. He had a pleasant speaking voice and narrated the 1944 film version of *Madame Curie*, again starring Greer Garson with Walter Pidgeon. In 1943 he published *The Story of Dr. Wassell*, an inspiring account of the rescue of wounded sailors from the U.S. cruisers *Houston* and *Marblehead* off the coast of Java. This was a new venture for Hilton, for *The Story of Dr. Wassell* is not a novel but a true account. Based on interviews with Commander Corydon Wassell himself and with some of the sailors who survived, the book is a moving story of heroism and dedication at a time when they were in imminent danger of being overrun by the advancing Japanese. In terse, simple prose Hilton relates the story of twelve badly wounded men, how they were cared for by Dr. Wassell and eventually transported safely to Australia. The film adaptation was directed by Cecil B. de Mille and starred Gary Cooper. Both book and film were highly praised at the time and did much to enhance Hilton's reputation. Another wartime venture was a series of radio broadcasts under the title "Ceiling Unlimited," containing his personal thoughts on the world conflict.

With the ending of the Second World War in 1945 Hilton decided to concentrate on his vocation as a novelist. He moved to a modest single story house at Long Beach, 25 miles south of Hollywood, and spent the remaining years of his life quietly writing. After his divorce from Galina Kopineck in 1945 he and his first wife Alice were reconciled and she remained his companion until his death. His parents had lived with him in California during the war years but his mother, Elizabeth, died there in 1943. (His father returned to Britain after the war and died at his home at Woodford Green in 1955, aged 83.) For a few years (1948–1951) he was host and editor of the "Hallmark Playhouse" series broadcast on the CBS network and traveled widely in the course of his radio activities, but the central focus of his life in his final decade was the writing of novels and short stories.

It is worth remembering that in addition to his work as a novelist and scriptwriter Hilton was an accomplished writer of short stories. Not all of them are of equal merit by any means but some are well worth rescuing from neglect. For example, "Twilight of the Wise" is a finely crafted tale describing an escape from a German prisoner of war camp during the First World War; "Appassionata" is a novella-length story relating the life and loves of a successful concert pianist; and "Shangri-La Is Where You Find It" (despite its title it has no connection with *Lost Horizon*) is another tender love story.

He also wrote a number of intriguing detective stories. These would be well worth collecting together in an omnibus volume.[36]

His Last Novels

So Well Remembered, published in the U.S. in 1945 and in Britain in 1947, is a long family saga set in the Lancashire mill town of Browdley, the same setting as in *And Now Goodbye*. It tells the story of an idealistic newspaper editor, George Boswell, who marries an attractive but unscrupulous woman, Livia Channing, the daughter of a man involved in a financial scandal. Livia is ambitious for success and is discontented with what she sees as the narrow horizons of Browdley; George is content to remain in the community he knows and loves. The struggle between their opposing temperaments and the impact this has on their family and friends is told in a narrative of absorbing interest. Possessive, intense and single-minded, Livia tries to shape George's life to meet her own ends. Good humored, stolid and modest, George at last sees through her true nature and is content to devote his life to human betterment. As a picture of English life between 1920 and 1940 *So Well Remembered* is a satisfying and thought-provoking read. It was favorably reviewed and was adapted for the screen in 1947, with John Mills as George Boswell and the American actress Martha Scott as Livia. The film was narrated by Hilton with a screenplay written by John Paxton. Filmed largely at Macclesfield in Cheshire, the screen version conveys the essence of the novel and is a fine example of a British film of the period. Mills and Scott are both excellent in their roles and Trevor Howard gives a memorable performance as a doctor fighting a diphtheria epidemic.

Nothing So Strange, published in 1948, is one of the least known and least discussed of Hilton's novels. The title is taken from a quotation by Daniel Webster: "There is nothing so powerful as truth — and often nothing so strange."

The story may be briefly summarized as follows: An American mathematician, Mark Bradley, who is an expert in the field of quantum mathematics, is invited to work in Vienna and Berlin in the late 1930s, under the tutelage of an eminent German scientist, Hugo Framm. In the worsening international situation it soon becomes clear to Bradley that Framm is increasingly drawn toward Nazi ideas, and that Framm is working on data connected with nuclear energy. Bradley senses that there is a real danger that Nazi Germany may develop an atomic bomb and does his utmost to frustrate this ambition. Knowing that he is trusted implicitly by Framm, and that Framm relies on him heavily for much of the "donkey work," he deliberately falsifies some mathematical results so as to mislead Framm and delay the German nuclear bomb project. He then returns to America and eventually obtains a post at Oak Ridge where he contributes to the Manhattan Project (the development of the atomic bomb by the United States in 1945). The novel ends with the detonation of the bomb over Hiroshima.

Expressed thus baldly, the plot sounds untypical of Hilton and rather more in the manner of Frederick Forsyth or John Le Carré. In fact it contains many characteristic Hiltonian touches. The novel is told in the first person by a female narrator, Jane Waring, a young writer who is attracted to Bradley and ultimately falls in love with him. Hilton really gets inside this character and as the novel proceeds more and more of her personality is revealed. The reader shares with the narrator her fascination with Bradley, her puzzlement at his enigmatic personality, her desire to find out more and more about his past, and her determination to help him overcome his phobias. Bradley himself is a complex character, consumed with the passion for scientific research but increasingly fascinated by Jane and drawn to her. Hilton communicates to the reader Bradley's obsession with the quest for scientific truth, yet at the same time one is aware of his need for human society and in particular his yearning for sympathetic understanding.

As one would expect in a Hilton novel there are many reflections about life and philosophy, and the great issues of war and peace. Most thought provoking, for example, is the comment that "in practice the use of atomic energy for destruction makes such a difference in degree that it constitutes a real difference in kind. For the first time in human history it becomes possible to destroy whole cities and populations in an instant." A perceptive observation in 1948![37]

Nothing So Strange is a stimulating and interesting read which vividly conveys the anxious atmosphere of the war years. It raises ethical and philosophical issues which are still highly relevant today. It tells a good tale in a fluent and entertaining way and deserves to be more widely known.

His next work, *Morning Journey*, published in 1951, is in my judgment the least successful of his later novels. Clearly intended as a panoramic novel embodying his reflections on Hollywood, it is the story of Carey Arundel, a gentle and outgoing girl who wishes to be an actress, and her destructive obsession with Paul Saffron, a dynamic and single-minded film producer. The contrast between her generous and loyal nature and the forceful personality of Saffron — a figure who suggests the mercurial character of Orson Welles — forms the substance of the story. Interwoven with her love-hate relationship with Saffron is the story of her involvement with the wealthy and possessive Austen Bond, a financier who claims to love her but deplores her previous liaison and her stage and screen career. The tangled narrative of the relationship between these three contrasting characters is played out against a background of the stage and movie world in America and Britain. Though favorably reviewed at the time *Morning Journey* lacks the readability of Hilton's other novels and suffers from an excessively wordy and convoluted plot. It is worth reading as a study of human nature and as a commentary on Hollywood as Hilton remembered it. It probably has few readers today but Carey Arundel — warm, humorous and steadfast — deserves to live as one of his most engaging and lifelike characters.

His last novel, *Time and Time Again*, appeared in 1953. It is in effect the autobiography of Charles Anderson, a British diplomat, who looks back on his life and career and reflects on the nature of happiness, looking on with chagrin at his son making the same mistakes he had made as a young man. It is an absorbing story with memorable characters including Charles himself— a man much in the mould of Conway in *Lost Horizon* and Rainier in *Random Harvest*— his wife, Jane Coppermill; his son, Gerald; and his father, Sir Havelock Anderson. The description of Charles's student days in Cambridge, his adolescent romance with Lily Mansfield and his encounter with Lily's father is particularly well realized and is for this reader the finest part of the novel. The intensity of an adolescent love affair is vividly conveyed, as is the contrast between Charles's youthful innocence and his father's cynicism. The later chapters recall the experience of living in London during the Second World War with descriptions of fire watching, air raids, searchlights, and the unforgettable atmosphere of that time.

Time and Time Again is one of the most carefully written of Hilton's novels. The manuscript reveals that the original typescript draft was heavily revised and corrected in ink, with multiple variant drafts of several scenes. Hilton clearly took great pains over the writing of the story, and the care with which he revised it suggests that the novel had a deep personal significance for him. In looking back on his life and career, skill-fully interwoven with the events of the twentieth century, Anderson mir-rors Hilton's own outlook on the world and presents a distillation of his gentle and tolerant philosophy.

In 1954 Hilton's health deteriorated. He had been feeling unwell for some time and had been diagnosed (mistakenly) as suffering from gall bladder trouble and arthritis. He traveled to London to visit friends and also to carry out research for a book he was writing (a biography of the Duke of Edinburgh, which was published after Hilton's death) but returned hurriedly to America when his ailment worsened. On November 21 he entered Seaside Hospital, Long Beach, where he was diagnosed as being terminally ill with cancer of the liver. He died on December 20, 1954, with his wife, Alice, at his bedside.

His friend Cyril Clemens wrote movingly of him:

> But the restless, groping spirit of James Hilton had perhaps fled the world of letters years ago. Whether it was Hollywood or success or indifferent health that sapped the fresh charm, who shall say? In the 1920's and 1930's his dream-misted pen skyrocketed him to popular fame. While he was not of the Nobel Prize school, he was understood, appreciated and probably read more than most of the Stockholm favorites. He possessed a fine craftsmanship and a humanity pricked by genuine pathos. Hilton's books were best sell-ers, for which a great deal more could be said by literary critics than they grudgingly afford.[38]

He was buried at Sunnyside Memorial Park, Long Beach, but follow-ing Alice's death in 1962 he was re-interred alongside her at Knollkreg Memorial Park, Abingdon, Virginia, apparently in accordance with her wishes. The inscription on his grave reads:

James Hilton

Author of   Lost Horizon   Goodbye Mr. Chips
Random Harvest   So Well Remembered
Creator of the word   Shangri-La

All things in moderation even the excess of virtue
itself he kept at heart and throughout all vicissitudes
the tranquil tastes of a scholar

It seems fitting that the inscription on his tomb should be a quotation from his finest work, *Lost Horizon*.[39]

A Man of His Time

To reflect on the life and work of James Hilton is to survey the literary scene of his time and the changing landscape of the English novel. He was born at a time when the "three decker" novel popular with the Victorians had come to an end and a new generation of writers including Wells, Bennett and Conrad was making its presence felt. He was fortunate in that the kind of novels he wished to write — stories of ordinary men and women whose lives are transformed by an unforeseen encounter or event — was then in fashion. His fiction was in the mood of its time: highly readable, fluently written, and the antithesis of such writers as Virginia Woolf and James Joyce. His generation of writers — Howard Spring, Francis Brett Young, H.E. Bates, Graham Greene, A.J. Cronin, John Steinbeck — produced some of the outstanding novels of their day and at their height commanded an audience of millions. And it can surely be no accident that the height of Hilton's fame coincided with the "golden age" of the Hollywood film industry. Following his death *The Times* stated: "From the first he had showed a talent for storytelling in a smooth and accomplished style and for the sharp delineation of character, two qualities which sell a novelist's works and help to turn them into films."[40]

Eight of his novels were adapted for the screen and three of these — *Lost Horizon, Goodbye Mr. Chips* and *Random Harvest* — are now regarded as classics of their kind. All three possess the qualities which help to define a successful movie adaptation: a good story, memorable characters, and themes with which viewers can identify. The fact that these films are still much in demand in video and DVD format demonstrates the continuing desire for movies of this caliber. It is fashionable to scoff at films of this kind as "Hollywood weepies" but there is undoubtedly a market for novels and movies expressing human emotions in a setting removed from gratuitous violence. Hilton was fourteen in 1914 and therefore belonged to a generation which could remember England as it was before the old world was destroyed forever in the mud and blood of Flanders. He knew that the old world had many faults but also knew that it possessed virtues, and that the values for which Britain stood — tolerance, fairness, democracy, free speech — were worth protecting. This is what he meant when he wrote in his "Chapter of Autobiography": "Time will bring regrets, if any. For myself, I do not object to being called a sentimentalist because I acknowledge the passing of a great age with something warmer than a sneer."[41]

The first half of the twentieth century was characterized by two world wars, immense social and economic upheavals, the beginnings of the Cold War and the dawn of the nuclear age. In a literary career spanning three decades Hilton encapsulated the hopes and anxieties of a generation of readers and, through the medium of his novels, mirrored their thoughts, concerns and aspirations. *Lost Horizon* expressed the longings of a generation weary of conflict and eager to embrace the promise of peace. *Random Harvest* mirrored the thoughts and feelings of thousands traumatized by war and dreading the ominous signs of another conflict. *So Well Remembered* presented a microcosm of life in an ordinary English town and neatly dramatized the tension between those who pursue their own ends and those who strive for human betterment. *Nothing So Strange* encapsulated the mood of the Cold War and the anxieties of the nuclear age. For all these reasons it could be argued that Hilton was essentially a man of his time, reflecting the hopes and fears of his generation.

From another standpoint it can be asserted that his work still has relevance for the 21st century. The issues with which he was concerned — war and peace, human happiness, human aspirations, the values by which we live — are timeless and as relevant today as in the 1930s. In an age when the trend is for dysfunctional, anxiety-ridden fiction with no strong narrative thread there may well be a renewed demand for novels cast in the solid tradition of Hilton and his contemporaries.

As we approach the 75th anniversary of the publication of *Lost Horizon* it is surely time to look again not only at this novel but the other novels of his maturity. Such novels as *And Now Goodbye, We Are Not Alone,*

Random Harvest, *So Well Remembered* and *Time and Time Again* are rich in portrayals of people and places drawn with affection and insight. These are not "recipe novels" filled with salaciousness or violence but reflective stories depicting the lives and loves of ordinary people. Hilton deserves to be remembered as the author of a number of finely crafted novels which have enriched our lives.

2

Content

Lost Horizon begins with a Prolog which "sets the scene" for the narrative that follows. The Prolog is told by an unnamed narrator who has attended the same school in England as Rutherford, a novelist, and Wyland, a diplomat. The three are dining together and the conversation turns to a former school friend of theirs, Conway, an exceptionally gifted and charismatic man. During their conversation it is revealed that Conway had been a passenger in a plane which had been hijacked a year previously (in May 1931) while en route from Baskul in Afghanistan to Peshawar in India. The plane had not returned and Conway had been reported as missing.

After the dinner Rutherford and the narrator continue their conversation at Rutherford's hotel. Rutherford explains that he knows Conway is not dead as he had met his old friend a few months previously. Conway had been a patient at a hospital in Chung-Kiang, China, where he had been very ill and had lost his memory. Gradually Conway had been nursed back to health and Rutherford had offered to accompany him back to England. While on board ship on the homeward journey, Conway had regained his memory and gave Rutherford a full account of his experiences in the hijacked plane and afterward. The regaining of his memory had been triggered by the fact that one of the passengers on the ship was Sieveking the pianist who had given a recital of Chopin pieces. After the recital Conway himself had begun to play the piano and Sieveking had asked what the piece was. Conway replied that the piece was a Chopin study. Sieveking, who was a Chopin expert, had denied this but Conway had been emphatic. Eventually he claimed that the piece was unpublished and had been taught him by a former pupil of Chopin's. Sieveking did not see how this was possible as Chopin had died in 1849.

Later Conway had told Rutherford the full story. He claimed to have been taken to a mysterious lamasery in Tibet called Shangri-La where the lamas lived to an advanced age and where there was a fabulous collection of books, music and works of art. After telling his story Conway then disappeared, but Rutherford was sufficiently impressed by the narrative to write it all down in the form of a manuscript. Rutherford explains that he sees no reason to believe the story but hands the manuscript to the narrator and urges him to read it. The narrator is warned that the story is a fantastic one but Rutherford is anxious to know what he makes of it.

Conway's story comprises Chapters 1–11 of the novel. Chapter One opens with a description of the hijacking of the plane at Baskul airport. There are four passengers on the plane: Conway himself; his deputy, Mallinson; Henry Barnard, an American citizen; and a woman missionary, Miss Brinklow. The four had expected to be conveyed from Baskul (where they are fleeing from a revolution) to Peshawar, but it becomes clear that the pilot is following an altogether different course. It is also apparent that the pilot is unfamiliar to them. Mallinson becomes increasingly alarmed but Conway tries to calm him down. After a long time the plane stops for refueling in a remote valley, but none of the passengers are allowed to leave the aircraft. The pilot then resumes his journey, declining all explanations or attempts at conversation. The plane journey continues for many hours, until at length it becomes clear that the pilot is heading toward a spectacular mountain range which the passengers assume to be in Tibet, a thousand miles away from where they expected to be.

In Chapter Two the plane journey continues. All four passengers manage to get some sleep but all are anxious and increasingly curious to know where the pilot is taking them. On awakening from sleep it is apparent that the engine has been cut off and they assume the fuel supply is exhausted. The plane makes a forced landing in a desolate, windswept valley. The passengers are unhurt but they find the pilot is unconscious.

He regains consciousness briefly and urges them to make their way to a nearby lamasery where they will find food and shelter. The pilot then dies, leaving them to spend the night huddled in the plane. In the morning they are about to start on their journey to the lamasery when they see coming toward them a party of Tibetans carrying a man in a hooded chair.

The third chapter contains an account of their journey to the lamasery of Shangri-La. The man in the hooded chair addresses them in English and explains that he is from the lamasery and that his name is Chang. Conway introduces himself and the others, and asks for directions for the journey. Chang insists that he and his party will guide them to the lamasery as it is not an easy journey.

The journey occupies the whole morning as they have first to ascend a steep valley and then be roped together in mountaineering fashion while they proceed along a hazardous path cut along the flank of a rock wall, with an abyss on one side. After what seems an exhausting journey they

Conway and his fellow passengers meet Chang and the emissaries from Shangri-La in the Frank Capra film version of *Lost Horizon* (courtesy R. Dixon Smith).

at last see the lamasery before them: a group of colored pavilions clinging perilously to the mountainside. The lamasery itself overlooks a lush valley, protected on all sides by mountains. It seems to Conway a pleasant, favored place, although extremely isolated. Dominating the lamasery and the valley is a high and symmetrically shaped mountain which Chang explains is called Karakal. The party are ushered into the lamasery buildings and Chang invites all of them to join him that evening for dinner. They accept the invitation, although Mallinson stresses he is eager to leave as soon as humanly possible.

The fourth chapter opens with a description of the dinner presided over by Chang. He explains that Shangri-La is an isolated community which receives very few visitors. Miss Brinklow makes enquiries regarding the underlying philosophy of the community and Chang explains that their prevalent belief is moderation in all things, with the lamasery embracing a number of different faiths and beliefs. Mallinson interrupts the philosophical discussion by demanding to know how they can return to the outside world as a matter of urgency. Chang replies that nothing could be arranged immediately, and after an angry exchange of words, Mallinson collapses from exhaustion.

Conway and Chang then have a private conversation in a calmer atmosphere. Chang states that none of them are in any danger at Shangri-La but that there cannot be any undue haste in making plans for their departure. During that dialog it becomes apparent that the arrival of the four passengers had been expected by the lamasery and Conway speculates on the significance of this.

The following morning, after an excellent breakfast, Chang again joins them. Mallinson immediately resumes the argument of the previous day and demands to know when porters can be found to escort them back to civilization. Chang explains that a party of porters is expected in about two months' time, and that in the meantime Shangri-La will extend its utmost hospitality to the visitors. Conway is prepared to accept the situation without argument, but Mallinson is extremely angry. He is dismayed at the prospect of having to remain at the lamasery for so long.

Chapter Five begins with the four visitors discussing their predicament and reluctantly concluding that they have no alternative but to remain at the lamasery for two months. Even Mallinson reluctantly agrees. Chang then offers to show them round the lamasery buildings and they accept his suggestion.

They are given a conducted tour of Shangri-La's buildings during which it becomes clear that the lamasery possesses extensive collections of works of art, music and books. During this tour they encounter a young Chinese girl who plays for them on the harpsichord. Chang explains that her name is Lo-Tsen and that she too aspires to enter the lamahood. The four are intrigued to know what a young girl is doing in a lamasery and how she came to be there.

That evening Conway strolls alone in the courtyards and thinks over all that has happened to him. While he is deep in thought he hears the sound of music and lamenting, and realizes he is listening to a funeral service. He overhears a conversation between two of the Tibetans from which it becomes apparent that the pilot who brought the passengers to Shangri-La has been buried and that his name was Talu. It is also clear that Talu was known to the lamasery inhabitants and that the air flight had been planned and carried out on the orders of Shangri-La's rulers.

In Chapter Six the party are given a conducted tour of the valley of Blue Moon. They are impressed with the evident happiness and goodwill of the valley population. Miss Brinklow decides to learn Tibetan and Chang lends her a book on the subject. Conway too finds much to interest him and spends pleasant hours in the library and in the music room. He continues to be intrigued by Lo-Tsen and both he and Mallinson speculate about her. Mallinson is irritated by Barnard's continual good humor and by chance discovers that Barnard's real name is Chalmers Bryant and that he is wanted by the police for alleged financial irregularities. That evening after dinner Barnard confesses to his real identity. Mallinson is highly critical of him and accuses him of blatant dishonesty; Conway is more tolerant and accepts that the Wall Street Crash and its aftermath were beyond Barnard's control.

Conway's thoughts then return to Shangri-La and all that it means to him. He realises that if the porters were to arrive he would not be overjoyed at seeing them as he had found contentment and happiness at the lamasery. He tries to imagine what the journey home would be like and what he will say in newspaper interviews. In the midst of his reflections Chang approaches him in a state of great excitement to tell him that the High Lama wishes to see him at once. Chang emphasizes that this is an unprecedented honor as guests are never received so soon after their arrival. Conway is then escorted to the High Lama's apartments.

The lengthy conversation between the High Lama and Conway forms the substance of Chapters Seven and Eight. The High Lama proves to be an old man in Chinese dress who welcomes Conway with grave courtesy. He proceeds to outline the history of Shangri-La from its earliest beginnings, stressing that the lamasery in its present form owes its inception to a certain Father Perrault, a Capuchin friar who had begun living at Shangri-La in the year 1734 at the age of 53. Perrault was a man of wisdom and enterprise who had been instrumental in establishing and leading a community based on both Christian and Buddhist principles. He became a revered figure, deeply respected by the lama and by the industrious folk in the valley below. In the year 1803 a European named Henschell had arrived at Shangri-La, attracted by stories of gold. Originally his intention had been to enrich himself but in time he found the atmosphere of the lamasery so attractive and so conducive to a life of peace and contentment that he decided to remain. Henschell devised the complicated system which enabled the lamasery to obtain supplies of books and artefacts from the outside world and pay for them with gold.

In the course of time other visitors arrived at Shangri-La and the hospitality of the lamasery was extended to them, subject to one important proviso. The High Lama then asks Conway to guess what that proviso is. Conway assumes that the proviso is that visitors who approach within a certain radius of the lamasery are made welcome, subject to the condition that they must remain permanently. He also guesses that Father Perrault is still alive, and that Perrault and the High Lama are one and the same.

Perrault explains that the proviso is essential and invariable, otherwise the precise location of Shangri-La would no longer be a secret. Once it became known that the lamasery existed and that it possessed not only gold but also art treasures there would be a danger of unwelcome visitors.

Conway enquires why he and his three companions have been brought to Shangri-La. The High Lama explains that since the 1914–1918 war and the Russian Revolution travel and exploration in Tibet have been almost non-existent, and in fact there had been no arrivals in Shangri-La since 1912. The number of inhabitants was dwindling and it was one of their own valley people, a young man named Talu, who had suggested the idea of bringing a group of people by plane.

Conway asks what is the point behind it all and Perrault replies that he foresees a disastrous world war in which all art and wisdom will be destroyed. Because of its remoteness Shangri-La may hope to survive such a conflict and would seek to preserve the wisdom and culture of the past against the day of a renaissance.

At the end of their meeting Perrault asks Conway not to divulge what he has said to Mallinson, Barnard and Miss Brinklow. Conway agrees, and in silence the two men part.

Chapter Nine opens with the inevitable chorus of questions from his three companions. They are naturally eager to hear what the High Lama is like, whether he can be trusted, and what was said about porters. Conway disappoints them all and at the earliest opportunity leaves them, wishing to be alone.

Chang now talks to him without reserve and answers many questions about the lamasery. Conway learns that he can expect a "probationary" period of five years at Shangri-La, after which he will probably live for half a century or more at the apparent age of forty. Chang explains that in his own case he had arrived at the lamasery in 1855 at the age of 22. There had been several instances where lamasery inhabitants had left the valley and had then suddenly aged, so clearly the unique atmosphere of the valley was essential to the retarding process.

During the next weeks Conway meets several of the lamasery inhabitants including a friendly German named Meister and a Frenchman named Briac who had been a pupil of Chopin. He also encounters a benevolent man who in his youth had once stayed at Haworth Parsonage and had met the Brontë sisters. Conway has a further meeting with the High Lama and begins to feel a sense of kinship with Perrault's mind and deep respect for his learning and judgment.

Chapter Ten, one of the longest chapters in the novel, is filled with incidents. It opens with an account of further meetings between Conway and the High Lama, who are now meeting with increasing frequency. These conversations range over history and philosophy, and Perrault tells Conway that he has never met his like before. Conway replies that the world war was a chastening and traumatic experience for those of his own generation.

Conway's world revolves around his meetings with Father Perrault, his attraction for the enigmatic Lo-Tsen and his arguments with the impatient and impulsive Mallinson. He reflects that he will be happier when his three companions know as much as he does about the lamasery. Miss Brinklow surprises them all by announcing her decision to remain at Shangri-La: she feels it is her duty to stay behind and establish a Christian mission there. Barnard also announces his decision to remain. Conway is increasingly concerned about Mallinson who is counting the days to the arrival of the porters. He seeks Chang's advice, who tells him that the porters *will* arrive but that Mallinson will find they are unable or unwilling to take him with them. Chang feels it would be a solution to the problem if Mallinson and Lo-Tsen would fall in love.

Meanwhile Conway himself is content. He likes the serene world of Shangri-La with its unhurried atmosphere, its books and music, and the calmness and industry of the lamas. Above all he is happy in the reflection that now at last he has the time to do what he wants to do without the distractions of the western world.

The High Lama tells Conway that the question of what to do about Mallinson is Conway's problem, not his. When Conway asks why, Perrault replies that he feels his own death is imminent and that he has decided to appoint Conway as his successor. He explains that he has been searching for a successor for a long time and has at last found a man who is young in years but wise in knowledge. Perrault foresees a war in which culture and beauty are trampled and all degenerates into chaos, but holds out the prospect of Conway presiding over a rejuvenated Shangri-La and a new world stirring in the ruins. The High Lama speaks eloquently of his vision of the future but when the speaking finishes Conway realizes that the aged priest has died. In a daze Conway leaves the High Lama's apartment, his mind awhirl with sorrow at the death and elation at his own succession. He becomes aware that Mallinson is waiting for him and that the youth is greatly excited.

2. Content

The following chapter opens with Mallinson breaking the news that porters have at last arrived and that he and Conway have until dawn to pack and leave. Lo-Tsen has made arrangements with the porters and is waiting for them five miles outside the valley. Mallinson urges haste in packing and preparation, but Conway — still dazed by the death of the High Lama — prevaricates. Conway then tells Mallinson the whole story of Shangri-La, including the fact that Lo-Tsen is in reality an elderly woman. Mallinson refuses to believe this and accuses Conway of being mad.

The two then argue about the situation, Conway trying to explain that they must remain at Shangri-La and Mallinson trying to find loopholes in his statements. Mallinson, in a rage, decides to leave on his own and the two say their farewells.

Some time later Mallinson returns, saying that he could not manage the mountain traverse alone and without being roped. He then breaks down in hysterics. When he is calmer the two men resume their discussion, with Mallinson asking a series of penetrating questions. What independent evidence has Conway for his assertion that the lamas can live to an advanced age? What proof has he that Lo-Tsen is not a young woman? Why does he believe what he has been told in a Tibetan monastery which he would not have believed in an English cathedral? Conway has to admit that these points are well made, and admits that in the end people believe what they wish to believe. Mallinson confesses that he has fallen in love with Lo-Tsen and is absolutely convinced that she is young.

Conway wrestles with his conscience for a long time, weighing up the competing considerations in his mind. On the one hand is his loyalty to Shangri-La, as well as the knowledge of his own succession and the attraction he feels for all that Shangri-La represents. On the other hand are his feelings for Mallinson, whom he genuinely likes, and his wish for Lo-Tsen's happiness. At last he reaches his decision and tells Mallinson he will come after all. The two men then leave Shangri-La and, after negotiating the hazardous traverse, meet up with Lo-Tsen and the porters. The porters are eager to begin the long journey to China.

At this point Conway's narrative ends.

The novel concludes with an Epilog in which Rutherford and the narrator of the Prolog meet again in Delhi and have a long talk about Conway's story. Rutherford asks whether he has read the manuscript and, if so, what he made of it. Rutherford emphasizes that the manuscript is based entirely on Conway's reminiscences and that he himself has added nothing. The narrator is noncommittal as to the veracity of the story, and Rutherford proceeds to outline his own attempts to establish its truthfulness or otherwise.

He has traveled widely in Afghanistan, India and China hoping to pick up clues as to Conway's whereabouts but has drawn a total blank. He was not allowed to enter Tibet though he did see the Kun Lun mountains in the distance. He had made determined efforts to find out more about Barnard, without success, and had also failed to discover anything more regarding Perrault or Henschell.

His next line of enquiry had been to try and discover what happened to Mallinson and Lo-Tsen after they left Shangri-La, and he had made exhaustive enquiries in an effort to uncover the truth. His own theory was that there had been some kind of tragedy and that Mallinson had failed to reach China. All that he had established was that Conway had been brought to Chung-Kiang by a Chinese woman. Was it possible that this woman was Lo-Tsen?

Eventually Rutherford had tracked down the doctor who had been at the mission hospital at Chung-Kiang and asked him if he remembered the Englishman who had lost his memory. The doctor recalled the case vividly, adding that the Chinese woman had been very ill herself and had died almost at once. Rutherford asked if the woman had been young, but the doctor replied that she had been "most old."

The novel ends with Rutherford and the narrator talking about Conway as they both remembered him, and of the strange unsolved mystery of Shangri-La.

3

Glossary

Lost Horizon was originally published in 1933. During the 75 years which have elapsed since then some of the words and phrases used by Hilton have changed their meaning or become obscure. Other terms, such as "Luft-Hansa machines," "tenner" and "Old Moore" may well require explication for the modern reader.

Page	Prolog
1	*Tempelhof*: The principal airport in Berlin, established in 1923.
1	*Tertius*: The third. Wyland Tertius is the third pupil with that surname to attend the school.
1	*M. V. O.*: Member of the Royal Victorian Order. The award is presented for outstanding public service.
1	*Luft-Hansa machines*: Hilton is referring to the Junkers G38, introduced in 1931, at that time the largest aircraft in the world. Each machine had four propeller-driven engines and had ample room for 30 passengers.
2	*Sibleys*: a flying suit designed for use in open cockpit aircraft.
2	*Baskul*: This is a fictitious name, apparently a disguised reference to Kabul, the capital of Afghanistan.
3	*Peshawur*: A city in Pakistan (then part of India) approximately 150 miles from Kabul. It is now spelt Peshawar.
5	*Jowett*: Benjamin Jowett (1817–93), a distinguished tutor at Balliol College, Oxford.

6   *D. S. O.*: Distinguished Service Order. This is a military decoration awarded for distinguished conduct in action.

6   *Don*: a Fellow of a College at a British University.

6   *F. O.*: Foreign Office.

7   *Philip Sydney*: English poet and soldier (1554–1586). The narrator describes Conway as "a bit Philip Sydneyish" because Conway excelled at both intellectual and practical pursuits.

8   *St Dominics*: Rutherford is referring to *The Fifth Form at St Dominics,* by Talbot Baines Reed, a popular school story published in 1881.

8   *Tit-Bits*: A popular British weekly paper, containing snippets of information and humor.

12   *Balliol*: One of the ancient Colleges of Oxford University.

14   *Sieveking*: Martinus Sieveking (1867–1950), notable pianist, who made extensive international tours.

17   *Weltschmerz*: distress at the condition of the world; nostalgic regret.

20   *Tertullian*: Carthaginian philosopher (circa 155–222), the first major Christian writer in Latin. The Latin phrase quoted by Rutherford, *credo quia impossible est,* means "I believe it because it is impossible."

Chapter 1

21   *Consul*: a senior government representative.

22   *tenner*: ten pounds sterling (£10.00). Hilton was writing in the 1930s when the purchasing power of the pound was considerably higher than it is today.

26   *Pushtu*: the language of the Afghans.

26   *Pathan*: one of the Afghan race who has settled in India.

37   *Jungfrau*: a spectacular mountain peak in Switzerland.

Chapter 2

38   *Nanga Parbat*: a Himalayan peak in North West Kashmir.

38   *Mummery*: Albert Frederick Mummery (1855–1895), British mountaineer and economist. He disappeared while attempting to climb Nanga Parbat.

3. Glossary

39   *Karakorams*: a mountain range forming the most northerly chain of the Himalayas.

42   *K 2*: the highest peak in the Karakorams, also known as Mount Godwin Austen (28,250 feet).

48   *Leitmotif*: a theme associated with a person or thought.

49   *Kuen-Lun*: One of the loftiest mountain ranges in Asia, the Kuen-Lun mountains (now spelt Kun Lun) form the north wall of the Tibetan plateau. The range runs generally west–east across Tibet, a total distance of some 2,300 miles.

51   *Afghans*: Miss Brinklow has been a missionary in Afghanistan.

53   *Shangri-La*: Hilton coined this term, which has since entered the English language. The publication of *Lost Horizon* in 1933 marked its first appearance. The term means literally "secret mountain pass."

55   *Saint Thomas of Canterbury*: Thomas à Becket (1118–70), archbishop of Canterbury, who was assassinated in Canterbury Cathedral on the orders of King Henry II.

Chapter 3

56   *lamasery*: a Tibetan monastery. A *lama* is a Buddhist priest.

59   *col*: a pass in a mountain range.

59   *couloir*: a gully.

65   *washing-mangle*: a manually operated device for squeezing water from garments by pressing them through rollers (since superseded by washing machines).

66   *Wetterhorn*: a spectacular triple-headed peak in Switzerland.

Chapter 4

80   *Blue Moon*: a moon that is blue is rarely seen, hence the phrase "once in a blue moon" means something which seldom occurs. *Blue Moon* was Hilton's original title for the novel.

81   *Henty*: G.A. Henty (1832–1902), a writer of adventure stories for boys.

82   *Whitaker*: an abbreviation for *Whitaker's Almanack*, a compendium of general information published annually since 1868.

85   *entrepôt*: a warehouse or store.

Chapter 5

Chapter 6

Chapter 7

3. Glossary

133   *Capuchin*: a friar of the Franciscan order.

134   *Malplaquet*: the battle of Malplaquet (1709) formed the conclusion of a series of victories by the Duke of Marlborough during a war between Britain and France.

135   *Gautama*: Gautama Siddhartha (563–483 BC), the founder of Buddhism.

140   *Om Mane Padme Hum*: a mantra in Tibetan Buddhism, usually translated as "oh jewel in the lotus."

145   *Tien-Shan*: a range of mountains in central Asia.

148   *you are still alive*: the events described in the story occur in the year 1931. Since Father Perrault was born in 1681 he is 250 years of age at the time.

Chapter 8

150   *Nordic*: the mainly Germanic peoples of North Western Europe.

157   *Grand Monarque*: King Louis XIV of France (1638–1715).

158   *Livy*: a Roman historian (59 BC–17 AD), whose history of Rome contained 142 books, of which only 35 survive.

158   *Summer Palace*: one of the ancient palaces in Peking (now Beijing), damaged by British soldiers during an uprising in 1900.

Chapter 9

163   *Dartmoor*: a large prison in Devonshire, England, normally for prisoners who have committed serious offences.

172   *Cortot*: Alfred Cortot (1877–1962), Swiss pianist who specialized in performing Chopin's works.

172   *Pachmann*: Vladimir Pachmann (1848–1933), Russian pianist and popular performer of Chopin's works.

Chapter 10

189   *Gibbon*: Edward Gibbon (1737–1794), English historian, author of *The Decline and Fall of the Roman Empire*.

189   *Spengler*: Oswald Spengler (1880–1936), German philosopher, author of *The Decline of the West*, which argued that civilizations pass through natural cycles of growth and decline.

191   *Rand*: the goldfield in South Africa.

Chapter 11

Epilog

4

Key to the Characters

Barnard, Henry D. Barnard is an American citizen, "a large, fleshy man, with a hard-bitten face in which good-humored wrinkles were not quite offset by pessimistic pouches." He arrives at Baskul from Persia and is one of the four passengers conveyed by airplane to Tibet. He accepts the situation with good humor and his three companions are puzzled when he expresses no desire to return. Later it transpires that he is traveling under an assumed name and that he is in reality Chalmers Bryant, a financier who is sought by the police for alleged irregularities. When Mallinson and Conway confront Barnard with this accusation he freely admits the truth, claiming that those who invested money in his enterprise in search of sudden riches were under an illusion. A mining engineer in his younger days, he decides to remain at Shangri-La, having been given permission by the authorities to prospect their gold deposits and make suggestions for improving yield.

Briac, Alphonse Briac is described as "a wiry, small-statured Frenchman, who did not look especially old, though he announced himself as a pupil of Chopin." He is a brilliant pianist and claims to know several Chopin compositions that have not been published. He teaches these to Conway, who spends hours memorizing them. Briac has only recently been initiated into the lamahood, and talks frequently about Chopin.

Brinklow, Miss Roberta   A small, leathery woman, Miss Brinklow is a missionary who has been practising in Afghanistan when she is forced to flee due to the revolution. She strongly disapproves of Shangri-La's philosophy of moderation and is convinced she has been sent there for a purpose. She makes the effort to learn Tibetan so that she can converse with the lamasery inhabitants in their own language. Together with Barnard she decides to remain at Shangri-La in the hope that she can influence the lamasery with her own religious views.

Bryant, Chalmers *see* **Barnard**

Chang   Chang is described as "an old or elderly Chinese, grey-haired, clean-shaven, and rather pallidly decorative in a silk embroidered gown." Originally a soldier by profession, he first enters Shangri-La in 1855 at the age of 22, having lost his way in the mountains while commanding troops operating against brigand tribes. Although extremely ill through cold and exhaustion he survives due to his youth and fitness. In the course of time he becomes a trusted confidant of the High Lama, becoming a senior figure at the lamasery. It is Chang's special function to meet all those who travel within a close radius of Shangri-La, to welcome them and escort them to the lamasery.

Chang is a wise, courteous and patient man who is solicitous for the welfare of the new arrivals. He has many conversations with Conway and does his utmost to explain anything Conway does not understand.

Conway, Hugh   Conway is a senior official in the British Consular service and has had a brilliant academic career, excelling at both school and university. After serving in the 1914–1918 war and being awarded a D.S.O. he became a don at Oxford, lecturing on Oriental History. In 1921 he commenced his diplomatic career, serving at several posts in China and Asia, though his heart is never in his work. In 1931 he is based at Baskul in Afghanistan and is one of a party of four transported by plane to Shangri-La.

From the outset he finds Shangri-La and its philosophy of calmness and moderation deeply attractive. He is increasingly intrigued by all that he sees and suspects he has been brought there by deliberate design. He regards it as a great honor to be received by the High Lama within weeks of his arrival, as Father Perrault does not normally see new arrivals until five years have passed. Conway has many conversations with the High Lama, and the two men come to respect and admire one another. Just before his own death Father Perrault appoints Conway as his successor.

Conway has a heated argument with Mallinson, who is eager to leave Shangri-La and return to England. At first Conway refuses to come with him, having decided to remain at Shangri-La. Eventually he relents and agrees to accompany Mallinson and Lo-Tsen in their journey. After appalling hardships, in the course of which both Mallinson and Lo-Tsen are presumed to have died, Conway reaches the Chinese town of Chung-Kiang. He is extremely ill and suffering from amnesia.

Gradually he regains his health and after some months, and with much help from Rutherford, he succeeds in regaining his memory. While traveling to the United States en route for England Conway tells Rutherford the full story of his experiences at Shangri-La but then gives his friend the slip. Rutherford presumes that Conway has decided to try to find his way back to Tibet and the lamasery.

Conway can be regarded as the most important character in *Lost Horizon* for it is his narrative which forms the substance of the novel and — if his story is to be believed — he is Perrault's appointed successor as the High Lama of Shangri-La. Both Rutherford and the neurologist remember Conway with great distinctness and recall his kindness, brilliance and charisma.

Doctor   A young Chinese Christian doctor, he is based at the mission hospital in Chung-Kiang where Conway is one of his patients. Later he is transferred to a larger hospital in Shanghai, where Rutherford interviews him. The doctor explains that Conway had been brought to the mission hospital by a woman, who had been "most old."

Henschell   Henschell is an Austrian of noble birth who had soldiered against Napoleon in Italy. He wanders through Russia into Asia in search of wealth and enters the valley of Blue Moon by accident in the year 1803. Initially he is attracted by the gold deposits but soon he falls under the spell of Shangri-La and decides to remain. He meets Father Perrault and the two become firm friends and allies. Henschell begins the collections of Chinese art and establishes the library, making a journey to Peking for this purpose in 1809. He devises the system which enables the lamasery to obtain books and artefacts from the outside world and pay for them with gold. He is an exceptionally gifted man and it is Perrault's opinion that Shangri-La owes as much to Henschell as to himself. Henschell is killed in 1857 when he is shot by an Englishman, angered on being told that visitors who enter Shangri-La cannot be permitted to leave. Just before his death Henschell is sketched by a Chinese artist; Father Perrault keeps the portrait and shows it to Conway.

High Lama *see* Perrault

Lo-Tsen   Born in 1866, Lo-Tsen is of royal Manchu ancestry. She arrives at Shangri-La in 1884, while traveling to Kashgar to meet her betrothed, a Turkestan prince. She is a skilled harpsichordist and prefers the music of formal, precise composers such as Bach, Corelli and Scarlatti. Both Conway and Mallinson find her quiet gentleness and beauty deeply attractive; Mallinson falls in love with her, convinced she is a young woman. Conway warns him that Lo-Tsen is in reality elderly and fragile but Mallinson refuses to believe this. When the three eventually leave Shangri-La Lo-Tsen suddenly becomes her true age.

Mallinson, Captain Charles   Mallinson is the British vice-consul in Afghanistan and is Hugh Conway's assistant. An ardent, impetuous young man, he is 24 at the time of the story and is therefore thirteen years younger than Conway. He is one of the party transported by plane from Baskul to Tibet but, whereas Conway accepts his fate with equanimity, Mallinson is increasingly alarmed and impatient. On arrival at the lamasery he is deeply suspicious and resentful, clearly mistrusting Chang and anxious to leave Shangri-La as soon as possible.

He disbelieves Conway's explanation regarding the longevity of the lamas and has no sympathy with Shangri-La's aims or philosophy. During his stay at the lamasery he meets and falls in love with the Manchu girl Lo-Tsen and eventually succeeds in escaping with her. He is not heard of again and has presumably failed to survive the rigors of the journey.

Meister, Friedrich Born in 1845, Meister is a German professor at Jena who visits Tibet in 1887. He enters Shangri-La in that year, the sole survivor of an exploring party. He is a genial man who speaks fluent English and is one of the first inhabitants of the lamasery to be encountered by Conway.

Mother Superior A charming nun at a French Roman Catholic convent in Chung-Kiang, the Mother Superior encounters Rutherford on a train and tells him of a mysterious English patient at the mission hospital there. She proudly shows Rutherford round the hospital, which is very competently run, and introduces him to the patient. She is greatly excited when Rutherford tells her that he knows the man. When she learns that Rutherford is a writer she is thrilled by the thought that she might appear in one of his books.

Neurologist The neurologist is the unnamed narrator of the Prolog and the Epilog. He had attended the same school as Rutherford, Wyland and Conway and is a guest at a dinner attended by the former two. The conversation turns to their acquaintance Hugh Conway, whom he and Rutherford remember with affection. Rutherford explains that although Conway has disappeared he is apparently still alive and hands to the neurologist a manuscript describing Conway's journey to Tibet and sojourn at Shangri-La. Later Rutherford and the neurologist meet again and discuss whether or not Conway's narrative can be true.

The neurologist is the author of a technical work on his own subject. He remembers Conway vividly and although inclined to be non–committal at first regarding the veracity of Conway's tale, his final question to Rutherford — "Do you think he will ever find it?"— reveals that he has at last come to accept it.

Perrault, Father (The High Lama) Born in the year 1681, Perrault is a Capuchin friar who sets out from Peking in 1719 seeking traces of Christianity in Tibet. His three companions perish on the journey but Perrault himself stumbles by accident into the valley of the Blue Moon, where he finds a thriving community. He is nursed back to health and is instrumental in establishing a Christian monastery overlooking the valley, where he resides for many years. The unique atmosphere of Shangri-La proves to be conducive to long life and Perrault becomes a wise and revered figure, presiding over a community incorporating elements from both Christian and Buddhist philosophies. The lamasery is hospitable to strangers, but it is a proviso that those arriving at Shangri-La must remain there permanently.

Perrault and Conway begin to meet with increasing frequency; Perrault is attracted by Conway's detachment and breadth of mind, and Conway respects Perrault's wisdom and foresight. At last the High Lama invites Conway to become his successor, but then he dies after seeing a vision of Shangri-La surviving a terrible world conflict.

Rutherford   A novelist by profession, Rutherford was at school with Conway, Wyland and the neurologist. While on holiday in China Rutherford encounters a Mother Superior of a convent at Chung-Kiang, who mentions a mysterious patient whom the nun believes to be English. To Rutherford's amazement the patient turns out to be his former school friend Conway. Rutherford talks to Conway, who has been extremely ill, and assists him in leaving China and traveling by ship en route for America. While on the ship Conway regains his memory and gives Rutherford a detailed account of his experiences at Shangri-La. Conway then gives Rutherford the slip but writes to him later to thank him.

Rutherford prepares a manuscript based on Conway's narrative and gives it to the neurologist to read. Months later Rutherford and neurologist meet again and discuss Conway's story. In the meantime Rutherford has tried to establish the truth of Conway's adventures but the evidence is inconclusive.

Sanders   Sanders is a pleasant, cheerful youth who, while working as a pilot, encounters Rutherford, Wyland and the neurologist at Tempelhof Airport. Sanders tells them of an incident at Baskul during the previous year when a British plane had been hijacked. Wyland is displeased with him for having revealed the story.

Sieveking   Sieveking is a concert pianist who is traveling by ship from Shanghai to Honolulu en route for the United States. While on board he

gives a piano recital, mainly of Chopin pieces as he is a Chopin special-
ist. Conway is in the audience and after the concert is over, plays some
pieces on the piano himself. Sieveking is greatly excited, as it transpires
the compositions are unpublished Chopin studies. Later the same night
Conway regains his memory, his recollection of the piano compositions
having triggered the end of his amnesia. Sieveking persuades him to record
the pieces, but Conway disappears before this can be done.

Talu   A native of the valley of Blue Moon, Talu is a young man who is
trustworthy and in complete sympathy with the underlying philosophy of
Shangri-La. He conceives the idea of learning to fly at an American aviation school and then returning to the valley by air, bringing with him
additional reinforcements. The plan is approved by the High Lama, who
gives Talu a free hand in carrying it out. Talu succeeds in transporting four
passengers to the valley but he loses his own life when the plane crashes
on arrival. The High Lama explains to Conway that Talu was an excep-
tional and talented man whose death is a tragic loss.

Wyland   Wyland is a diplomat at the British Embassy in Berlin. A prig-
gish, formal man, he entertains Rutherford and the neurologist to dinner
at Tempelhof Airport. He had known Conway at school and university,
and regarded him as "clever, but rather slack." Later Rutherford is highly
critical of Wyland, who he believes is full of self-importance and has "the
complete head-prefectorial mind."

5

Reception

There can be no question that Hilton had high hopes for the success of *Lost Horizon*. He wrote later: "There is certainly no book of mine whose success I ever desired more keenly, for *Lost Horizon* was, in part, the expression of a mood for which I had always hoped to find sympathizers."[1] Given the fact that he had written and revised the novel with great care, that this was his first book to be published under the Macmillan imprint and that he had awaited publication with high expectations, he must had read the reviews with even more of his customary eagerness.

British Reviews

One of the first reviews to appear was published in the *Times Literary Supplement*, which was (and continues to be) one of the leading British literary journals. The article begins by praising Hilton's gifts as a storyteller:

> In earlier books Mr. Hilton has proved amply his possession of the storyteller's gift of continuous new invention, always adequately and often brilliantly clothed in the flesh and blood of convincing circumstance.[2]

The review goes on to criticize the novel on the grounds that the fantasy elements in the story are not fully realized. In particular the reviewer finds it incredible that a lamasery as elaborately equipped as Shangri-La could exist in a remote part of Tibet. In his view the concept of Shangri-La is too sketchy and facile to be fully convincing, though he concedes that "the book makes, if in its conception rather than its execution, the most of its opportunities." The review concludes with a paragraph which neatly summarizes the novel's strengths and weaknesses:

> Mr. Hilton always writes well and with imagination; his characters are clearly drawn and revealed in constant dramatic movement; his dialogue is excellent. He does, however, having created a situation, rather get out of it than resolve it; and one is not entirely convinced by Conway's final return to action, nor is the rather abrupt ending really satisfactory.

This is an important review which must have given Hilton satisfaction and also food for thought. Printed in a prominent position on the review page — coming below William Faulkner's *These Thirteen* and above Mazo de la Roche's *The Master of Jalna*— the article provides a balanced assessment of the novel and does not hesitate to give praise where praise is due. At the same time the reviewer shrewdly highlights those aspects of the book that are open to criticism, focusing in particular on the abrupt conclusion which arguably leaves many problems unresolved.

Under the heading "A Land of Eternal Youth," Margaret Pope in the *Daily Telegraph* described the book as "a fascinating story of high adventure." Following a summary of the novel's main themes her review concluded:

> He has drawn a lovely picture of a region inviolate, a place of delight where the spirit is enfranchised, the bonds unloosed.... Conway's dream dissolves like all too lovely things, at the first touch of reality, but while it lasted it was a thing of beauty.[3]

The Daily Telegraph's twice weekly book reviews page was highly respected in literary circles and for some years Hilton himself contributed regular reviews to the paper. The appraisal by Margaret Pope is therefore significant, especially as she praised the book so warmly, describing it as "a book to handle with gratitude."

Reviewing the book in the literary weekly *Everyman* the writer and critic Sir John Squire began his appraisal by deploring the cynicism and shallowness of so many contemporary novels, while acknowledging that cynicism was the fashion of the moment. He went on:

> It is an agreeable change to come across a book which is beautifully written, infused with poetry, and full of exciting adventures, both physical and intellectual ... all the various elements — psychological, conversational and pictorial — are exquisitely blended.... It is the sort of book one will probably re-read every year or two.[4]

This review is important for several reasons. Sir John Squire was an influential figure in the London literary scene and had a wide reputation as a critic, editor and poet; his views were therefore respected. Secondly, the review highlights the novel's literary and imaginative qualities, drawing attention to its craftsmanship and implicitly contrasting it with other fashionable novels of the day. Thirdly, by stressing that readers will wish to return to *Lost Horizon* at frequent intervals it reinforces the novel's claims to be regarded as a work of literature. Squire was the leader of a group of writers who shared an antipathy to "modernist" fiction — as exemplified by the works of Virginia Woolf and James Joyce — and he published several volumes of parodies.

Critics described him and his circle as "the Squirarchy," but there can be no doubt that he was a powerful figure in Fleet Street and he was an important ally for Hilton to have made.

A review in the distinguished magazine *Time and Tide* written by the novelist Francis Iles described the novel as "a provocative and thought making book." The reviewer stated:

> I read the book at a sitting, and enjoyed it thoroughly. The four visitors, each representing a different point of view, are convincingly drawn; and Conway, in whom we are most interested, is a clever study.[5]

However, the article's main criticism of *Lost Horizon* is that in Iles's judgment Hilton dwells too much on the theme of war and war neurosis. Iles claims that "the sad truth is that the war, for most of those in the front line, was just devastatingly boring" and takes Hilton to task for exaggerating its impact upon Conway. This, in the reviewer's opinion, mars the novel by making Conway's reaction to the war seem hysterical. But the review concedes that the novel contains "some very pretty philosophy" and concludes that as a whole the book is excellent.

Time and Tide was at its peak of popularity in the 1930s and was publishing work by leading American and European writers. To be reviewed in such a journal was quite a coup for Hilton, especially when one reflects that at that time his name was still not widely known.

In a warm tribute in the *Sphere* the novelist Cecil Roberts described the book as "a tour de force of the imagination." After describing the main elements of the story Roberts praised the book in these terms:

> The mystic exaltation found in the high altitude of the lamasery pervades the pages of this book and holds the reader in a trance of eager delight. Extravagant praise is the vice of the age, yet I would not hesitate to use superlative adjectives in describing this book.[6]

The *Sphere* was a popular weekly magazine with a large circulation and reached a far wider readership than those attained by literary and academic journals. To receive such a fulsome tribute in this publication, and from such a well known writer, was therefore highly encouraging, particularly as Roberts nominated Hilton as "likely to march in the front rank and uphold the tradition of English fiction."

Of all the reviews in British journals the one which must have given James Hilton especial gratification was the one which appeared in *The Bookman* for December 1933. After reviewing the books published during the past year the Editor concluded:

> The novel which I have read with most pleasure is James Hilton's *Lost Horizon*, a book which, with masterly economy, creates its own world; which is bold enough to use hackneyed situations and clever enough to turn them into something original; in which the story and the philosophy are intertwined, so that the first carries the reader rapidly forward, while the second remains as a quiet but persistent memory.[7]

The Bookman was a respected literary monthly founded in 1891. The fact that its editor, Ross Williamson, nominated *Lost Horizon* as the novel he had read with most pleasure during the past year is a significant recommendation. It is also notable that once again the review focuses on the manner in which story and philosophy are skillfully intertwined, and that *Lost Horizon* is one of those rare novels which "creates its own world."

American Reviews

Under the heading "Some Leading Autumn Fiction" the critic James W. Poling appraised the novel in the *New York Herald Tribune*. After summarizing the novel's main themes Poling drew attention to a possible weakness in the story by stating that the characters "frequently cease to be individuals and become instead mental concepts. And so the book is not completely convincing." Poling argues that the characters are not fully realized and that they tend to run to type. However, this criticism is balanced by praise for the novel's originality and for its literary qualities. The review concludes:

> Not that the novel hasn't much to offer, the gold outweighs the alloy. There are several truly dramatic moments, some moments of quiet beauty and others of pleasant satire and humor. The idea behind the book and its implied philosophy are mentally provocative, and it is all told in the same terse and imaginative prose which distinguish the author's earlier work.[8]

On the whole Hilton must have been well pleased with this review. While Poling's critique tends to pigeonhole the book as "escapist" literature it offers a balanced appraisal of the novel as a whole and draws attention to its strengths from a literary standpoint in addition to its philosophical elements.

Reviewing the book in the *Saturday Review of Literature* George Dangerfield stated that Hilton had joined "those many writers who have made the alluring and usually fatal journey into Xanadu." Dangerfield asserts that the borderline between realistic fiction and fantasy is very narrow and that too many authors fall into the trap of describing situations that are implausible or fortuitous. After praising Hilton for not falling into this trap the review summarises the novel's strengths and weaknesses:

> Mr. Hilton, as an Anglo-Saxon writer, is inclined to treat this
> place and its inhabitants with an exaggerated courtesy; his fantasy
> is sometimes to studiously delicate, too ponderously fragile. But
> only sometimes. The enjoyment of fantasy is not a matter of belief
> but acquiescence, and it is all to Mr. Hilton's credit that for the
> most part we are quite willing to acquiesce.[9]

Dangerfield warns against taking the novel too seriously, for in his view it is a "diversion," written simply to entertain. However, he concludes his review on a positive note by stating: "It quite definitely establishes Mr. Hilton as a writer to read now and to watch for in the future."

An unsigned critique in the *Yale Review* focused on the personality of Conway, describing him as "the roving Englishman of the Larger Dispensation" and drawing attention to the fact that he is weary not only of the war and its "bankrupt peace" but of the whole Western system with its emphasis on material values. The reviewer concludes with the observation that there is some humor in the novel but that

> The book is in the main a grave one — saved from the ponderous-
> ness which often infects such attempts by the simplicity and grace
> with which it is written. Altogether, like the author's first novel,
> *And Now Goodbye*, it is an unusual and refreshing work to come
> upon.[10]

An anonymous review in the *New York Times* describes the novel as "a mixture of Wellsian fantasy, Eastern mysticism and an adventure yarn" but concludes that the characters are vaguely realized and that there is a synthetic quality about the story:

> It is engagingly written for the most part, it is often effective, but
> it seems to be a little more than an intellectual tour de force.[11]

The review makes the same point as the *New York Herald Tribune*: that the story is well written and carefully thought out but that there is something lacking in the creation of the characters — they are not wholly convincing as flesh and blood men and women. The review finds the structure of the book inept, and feels that the prologue and epilogue are inadroit. However, the appraisal concludes with the observation that "what remains in the memory of the reader is a delicately imaginative picture of the lamasery and its ideals."

M.C. Bodwell in the *Canadian Forum* described *Lost Horizon* as an "excursion into the realms of pure fantasy." After summarizing the story and describing it as "an absorbing tale" his review encapsulates the novel in these terms:

> The plot is skilfully and lightly managed, and the characterization adequately convincing, though the bromidical Miss Brinklow is, perhaps, too well done. It is pleasant to discover such a well written novel which aims no higher than the laudable purpose of amusing its readers, and so entirely succeeds in its attempt.[12]

In the main the American and Canadian reviews took the view that *Lost Horizon* was written simply as an entertainment and that it would be a mistake to take it too seriously. Nearly all the reviewers concurred that the story is well executed and is worth reading but that the portrayal of the leading characters left something to be desired.

Critical Trends

We can now identify the main trends of criticism emerging in the months following publication of *Lost Horizon*. There is, first, a recognition that the novel is important and original, that it stands out from so much contemporary fiction by virtue of its literary quality.

Secondly, a number of critics drew attention to possible weaknesses in the story in the sense that the leading characters are arguably not fully realized and that they are *intellectual* rather than physical creations. Thirdly, some critics drew attention to narrative implausibilities and that the abrupt ending leaves too many problems in the air.

The critics were, however, agreed on one point — that *Lost Horizon* merits close attention as a work of fantasy in which philosophical and narrative elements are combined in a satisfactory whole. Whatever their reservations as to the feasibility of the concept of Shangri-La, all had to admit that the novel stood out from the crowd for the sheer quality of its writing and the originality of its central theme.

On the whole Hilton had good reason to be satisfied with the novel's reception. Despite some reservations as to the portrayal of the characters and the basic structure of the story, the critics were unanimous in praising the novel for the beauty of its prose, recognizing that Hilton was emerging as an important writer. The year 1933 was indeed a turning point in his life.

Not only was he now accepted as a Macmillan author and a novelist of note but later that same year he wrote the work which was to bring him fame and fortune: *Goodbye Mr. Chips*. The sales of this book led to increasing interest in his work and helped enormously to stimulate sales of *Lost Horizon*. From now onwards he was no longer a journalist living from hand to mouth but a respected novelist. He had "arrived" as a literary figure.

6

Texts

The publishing history of *Lost Horizon* is an intriguing case study in its own right, for it is the story of a novel whose sales were only modest initially but which soon became firmly established as a modern classic. A novel submitted by a little known author became in time a standard text known throughout the English speaking world and beyond.

Publication

The novel was first published in September 1933 by Macmillan in London and William Morrow in New York. Both Macmillan and William Morrow are long established and respected publishers and the young James Hilton must have had high hopes for the success of his book. On the dust jacket of their edition Morrow stated:

> *Lost Horizon* is being published simultaneously in England and America. The story is of such a character that it should not only definitely establish the author's reputation as a novelist, but add considerably to his already substantial group of followers.

To Hilton's disappointment sales of the novel were frustratingly slow. Despite some favorable reviews and one or two notable advocates sales seemed to stall and he was fearful that the book would soon be forgotten.

Then in June 1934 *Lost Horizon* was awarded the prestigious Hawthornden Prize, which is awarded annually for the best piece of imaginative writing published during the preceding year by a British author under the age of 41. Hilton wrote later: "The result was in the nature of a resurrection; the sale of the original English edition began to gather momentum, while in America the publishers took the almost unique step of issuing the book afresh."[1]

In October 1934 Morrow issued the "Hawthornden Prize Edition" of the novel with a special new jacket and a new binding, announcing that they intended to spend $1,000 in advertising the novel during the month of October. Advertising commenced in the *New York Times* and *Herald Tribune,* and in New York and Boston dailies. By May 1936 the Hawthornden Prize Edition had been reprinted fifteen times and had sold in excess of 70,000 copies.

In October 1936 Morrow issued the "Author's Edition" of *Lost Horizon* in a handsome new binding and with attractive colored illustrations by the artist Dan Grossbeck. Hilton contributed a specially written Preface for this edition, summarizing its publishing history and expressing his hopes for the novel's success.

It should be noted that the U.S. edition differs slightly from British editions. Apart form obvious differences such as American spelling and "gasoline" instead of "petrol," there is an interesting textual difference in the opening sentence. The British edition reads as follows:

> Cigars had burned low, and we were beginning to sample the disillusionment that usually afflicts old school friends who meet again as men and find themselves with less in common than they used to think.

The U.S. edition reads:

> Cigars had burned low, and we were beginning to sample the disillusionment that usually afflicts old school friends who have met again as men and found themselves with less in common than they had believed they had.

Readers will have their own preference as to which version they prefer. It is a difference in tense which slightly alters the perspective of the opening.

Other textual differences between the British and U.S. editions are as follows:

U.S.	British
From a colonnade steps descended to a garden, in which a lotus pool lay entrapped ... (page 97)	From a colonnade steps descended to a garden, in which by some tender curiosity of irrigation a lotus pool lay entrapped....
He could not quite determine whether she played merely for pleasure (page 111)	He could not quite determine whether she musicked merely for pleasure

Hardback Editions

Meanwhile Macmillan in London issued *Lost Horizon* in a variety of hardback editions, including a standard edition issued at seven shillings and sixpence (then the usual price for a new novel), a cheap edition at two shillings and a leatherette edition at two shillings and sixpence. In October 1936, simultaneously with Morrow's "Author's Edition," Macmillan launched the novel in a new format within "The Cottage Library." The Cottage Library was a series of classic novels issued in a pocket-sized format in imitation leather.

The pages had rounded corners and a pleasing typeface (my own copy with the pages slightly browning with age, now has a certain period charm). Other titles in the series included Lewis Carroll's *Alice in Wonderland,* Thomas Hardy's *Far from the Madding Crowd,* Rudyard Kipling's *Captains Courageous* and Hugh Walpole's *The Cathedral.* Macmillan kept *Lost Horizon* in this series until at least 1946, reprinting it six times over a ten year period. The 1937 reprint is particularly desirable as it has an attractive dust jacket featuring scenes from the film version and a quotation from Frank Capra describing the book as "one of the most important pieces of literature in the last decade."

In 1949 the novel was reissued by Macmillan as one of the titles within the Modern Fiction Library, and remained in this format for many years. The text was not reset for this edition but it was handsomely rebound with the addition of a dust jacket designed by Virginia Smith and featuring a photograph of Hilton. In describing the book the jacket text stated:

> Ever since its first appearance in 1933, *Lost Horizon* has been loved
> by thousands, both as a best selling novel and as a highly successful
> film.... This is not surprising, since for suspense, originality of
> theme, and dreamlike excitement it is unsurpassed.

Macmillan's sister companies in other lands were also producing their own editions. Commencing in 1943 the Macmillan Company of Canada, for example, issued a pocket-sized edition with an attractive dust jacket (showing the lamasery buildings perched on a mountainside) and a three-page note at the end, "About the Author," summarizing Hilton's life and literary career.

During the following decades *Lost Horizon* continued to be immensely popular, its sales stimulated by mass market paperback editions and by the huge fame of the Frank Capra film version. Translations into other languages soon appeared, including French (1943), Spanish (1944), Swedish (1948) and Japanese (1950). By the time of Hilton's death in 1954 "Shangri-La" had become a household name.

As the twentieth century drew to its close a number of fine editions of the novel were produced. In 1991 Pan Books of London published a well designed hardback edition, specially produced for Shangri-La Hotels and Resorts. Attractively bound in durable green covers, each copy had a dust jacket embossed with gilt lettering and featuring an illustration of a dreamlike scene of mountains and valleys wreathed in clouds. Each copy contained the statement: "This captivating story you are about to read was written in 1933 by an English novelist who wrote of an idyllic settlement high in the mountains of Tibet. Today, even amongst those who have never heard of *Lost Horizon,* the word 'Shangri-la' stands as a synonym for paradise." The hotel chain also produced a series of attractive book marks featuring extracts from the novel.

In 1996 William Morrow, the publishers of the original U.S. edition, took the unusual step of reissuing the novel as a facsimile hardback edition. This reproduces the dust jacket of the 1933 printing, even replicating wear and tear to give the appearance of a much read book. The jacket "blurb" states:

> We believe that this new novel *Lost Horizon,* is the finest thing
> Hilton has written. It has all the emotional, dramatic appeal of *And
> Now Goodbye,* the rich imaginative vision of *Ill Wind,* and the
> fulfillment of brilliant intellectual maturity promised in both these
> earlier books.

This is a desirable edition printed on high quality paper with a durable binding and a typeface which is a pleasure to read. It is an edition which many Hilton collectors will wish to have on their shelves.

Meanwhile in Britain the Reader's Digest Association published an attractive hardback edition of *Lost Horizon, Goodbye Mr. Chips* and *To You, Mr. Chips,* bound together in one volume. This has evocative color illustrations by the American artist Robert Andrew Parker, who had actually visited Tibet and based his illustrations on his sketches of the Tibetan landscape. The painting of the passengers setting out on their journey to Shangri-La from the crashed airplane is particularly striking. Like the Morrow edition, this has an excellent typeface and is printed on the finest quality paper, with the addition of a gilt embossed binding which would do justice to any of the classics of English literature. (It should be noted that though the book is printed in the United States the text is that of the British edition).

This text has the added bonus of an Afterword by Leonée Ormond, Professor of Victorian Studies at King's College, University of London. This provides a scholarly introduction to the novel which points out that "*Lost Horizon* is part of a long tradition of Utopian fiction in which characters find themselves in a strange and idealized world." Professor Ormond admirably surveys the novel's themes and motifs, underlining the links with *Goodbye Mr. Chips* and drawing the reader's attention to its philosophical elements.

Altogether this is a really sumptuous edition which any Hilton collector would be pleased to have. It is significant because it makes *Lost Horizon* available in a permanent form and also because the Afterword, written by a distinguished academic, demonstrates that Hilton is an important writer whose work merits serious attention. This is refreshing at a time when the prevailing attitude towards him is that he was a "middlebrow" novelist who wrote stories simply for entertainment.

Paperback Editions

In the United States Pocket Books of New York began issuing *Lost Horizon* in April 1939. By 1969 the publisher had reprinted the novel 70 times and sold two million copies of that one title alone, describing it as "one of the most beloved of all modern novels." Pocket Books editions of *Lost Horizon* are worth looking out for as they invariably have attractive cover illustrations and are well bound. (Modern copies often have "the first paperback ever published" printed on the cover, which seems puzzling as there have been paperbacks in Britain since at least the 1880s. What the publisher means is that this edition of *Lost Horizon* is the first paperback edition *of that novel* ever published: this statement is true as the Pocket Books edition preceded the Pan edition in Britain by 8 years). Pocket Books also issued paperback editions of two other Hilton novels, *Random Harvest* and *So Well Remembered,* and these too are highly collectable.

Pocket Books continued to reprint *Lost Horizon* at regular intervals in its Classics series and has now reissued the book no fewer than 106 times. The cover text describes Shangri-La as "a land of mystery and matchless beauty, where life is lived in tranquil wonder, beyond the grasp of a doomed world." By issuing the book in a pleasing format at a price of $6.99 the publishers have helped to ensure that *Lost Horizon* reaches a readership of millions. The cover design of lofty Shangri-La architecture against a background of shimmering mountains and an approaching airplane is enticing, while the heading WELCOME TO SHANGRI-LA on the back cover will arouse the curiosity of many readers.

In Britain, commencing in June 1947, the then newly launched firm of Pan Books issued the novel in a handy paperback format at the price of one shilling and sixpence. The Pan edition had a cover illustration by an anonymous artist showing lamasery buildings perched on a precipitous mountain range. Pan continued to reprint *Lost Horizon* for many years, with a variety of cover designs. When a second film version was made in 1973 a "tie-in" edition was produced featuring scenes from the film. There was also a special edition produced for Shangri La Hotels. Common to nearly all Pan Editions is the phrase "unsurpassed for haunting enchantment and originality of theme," which appears on the back cover of most editions. By the 1970s at least 400,000 copies had been sold in Pan Editions alone.

The Pan paperback editions are sought after by collectors for a number of reasons. The paperbacks of the 1940s often have cover designs by notable artists including Bip Pares (who also designed covers for *Random Harvest* and *So Well Remembered*), Edward Bawden and Carl Wilton. They were well produced, with a sturdy binding and good quality paper — except in the very early years when wartime paper restrictions were still in force. Pan's decision to have a pictorial cover for each of their publications was in marked contrast to Penguin, whose founder Allen Lane frowned on pictorial covers and refused to have them on Penguin editions, regarding them as a "gimmick." There can be no doubt that Pan's covers were eye-catching, especially when seen in a bookshop window display.[2]

Lost Horizon was in fact among the first titles Pan produced, the other early titles being *Ten Stories* by Rudyard Kipling, *Trilby* by George du Maurier, *The Small Back Room* by Nigel Balchin and *Three Time Plays* by J.B. Priestley. These early titles are keenly sought by both Pan collectors and Hilton enthusiasts.

In 1954 Macmillan issued a paperback edition of a simplified text of *Lost Horizon,* adapted and abridged by E.F. Dodd, with Hilton's permission. The Preface states that "this book is intended for use as a supplementary reader in the higher forms of secondary schools, particularly where English is taught as a second language." Dodd's simplified version retells the story in a vocabulary of two thousand words, while retaining the literary style of the original novel as far as possible. This edition contains a number of well drawn illustrations and has a striking cover design showing the four airplane passengers approaching Shangri-La (though, oddly enough, all four are dressed as if on a day out in fashionable New York!). This edition can be recommended to students who find Hilton's language or sentence structures difficult, especially as it contains explanatory notes and questions. It has been frequently reprinted.

The year 2003 marked the 70th anniversary of the first publication of *Lost Horizon*. To mark the occasion the British publisher Summersdale issued a "70th Anniversary Edition" with an appealing cover design in different shades of mauve depicting mysterious mountain ranges merging into a brilliant sunlit sky. The front cover announces the book as "The classic tale of Shangri-La," while the rear cover text states: "Summersdale are delighted to be re-releasing *Lost Horizon*, first published in 1933 and greeted with enormous critical and public acclaim." This is a handsome edition which does justice to a well loved text. With its clear typeface, good quality paper and eye-catching cover painting Summersdale deserve credit for having taken pains to re-issue the novel at a time when the prevailing fashion was for "Aga sagas" and blockbuster tales of crime and violence. The Anniversary Edition, which has already been reprinted, should ensure that *Lost Horizon* continues to be available in British bookshops for many years to come.

Collecting Hilton

Paperback editions of Hilton's novels are well worth collecting in their own right: many have attractive cover designs and some contain useful biographical information about the author. One of the reasons why paperback copies of *Lost Horizon* are so collectible is that the cover illustrations offer a fascinating insight into artists perceptions of the novel. Common to the Pan, Pocket Books and Summersdale editions is the idea of mountain ranges with their suggestion of mystery and inaccessibility. Other motifs depicted include the figure of Chang in his hooded chair, the aged High Lama, the enigmatic Lo-Tsen, lush vegetation hidden among barren wastes, and figures in Tibetan dress. Each generation of illustrators brings to the task their own interpretation of the novel's themes.

Printing technology has advanced considerably since *Lost Horizon* was first published, and modern editions such as those by Pocket Books and Summersdale are a world removed from the editions of the 1940s with their inferior quality paper. The fact remains, however, that to a book collector some of the older editions are much prized. The Macmillan Cottage library, for example, with its clear typeface, sturdy binding and durable paper is an excellent edition to have. *Lost Horizon* is a classic text and deserves to be read in an edition of the finest quality.

6. Texts

Among the changing vagaries of literary fashion one thing seems certain. As we approach the 75th anniversary of the novel's publication it is safe to assert that of all the books Hilton wrote it is *Lost Horizon* which seems certain to achieve classic status. This short tale, written in six weeks in the spring of 1933, will carry his name forward into the new millennium.

7

Contexts

Lost Horizon was published at a momentous time. The year 1933 saw Hitler coming to power in Germany, the Japanese invasion of China and the New Deal in the U.S. It also saw the publication of Orwell's *Down and Out in Paris and London,* the formation of the Odeon cinema circuit, the discovery of electrons and the first flight around the world. The novelists John Galsworthy, George Moore and Anthony Hope all died in that year. It was a year of unrest, widespread unemployment and increasing disillusionment following the high hopes of the League of Nations and post-war reconstruction. At the same time, 1933 was a time of innovation in literature and the arts with a new spirit of enquiry and experiment.

The Literary Background

The 1920s had been a period of experimentation in the European novel. James Joyce's *Ulysses* was published in 1922, Frank Kafka's *The Trial* and Virginia Woolf's *Mrs. Dalloway* in 1925, Herman Hesse's *Steppenwolf* in 1927 and D.H. Lawrence's *Lady Chatterley's Lover* in 1928. T.S. Eliot's *The Waste Land* (1922) reflected the disillusionment of the post-war generation and paved the way for a new mood in literature. While many novelists were content to produce material in the conventional pattern (J.B. Priestley's *The Good Companions* appeared in 1929), there was clearly a spirit of innovation abroad. Writers were seeking for new departures, for a fresh sense of direction in a world in which the old order was visibly passing away.

Alongside this urge to experiment there was a mainstream of writing in the solid English tradition. The popular novelists of the moment were Warwick Deeping, A.S.M. Hutchinson, Mary Webb and A.J. Cronin, all of whom were producing solid, well crafted novels on the traditional pattern. In the same month that *Lost Horizon* was published Macmillan also published *Master of Jalna* by Mazo de la Roche and *Vanessa* by Hugh Walpole. Hilton's new novel therefore appeared at a time when two differing strands were evident in the English novel. On the one hand was the innovative novel as exemplified by such writers as Joyce and Woolf; the novel which draws attention to its own fictionality, in which there is no reliable narrator, no chronological order and no neat tidying up of loose ends in the concluding chapter: the "modernist" novel. On the other hand was the long established tradition of writing a novel which tells a story, in which there is an omniscient narrator and a tidy conclusion bringing events to a resolution: the "realist" novel. Hilton's skill lies in the fact that *Lost Horizon* straddles both traditions. It *is* a conventional story in the sense that it describes the experiences of a group of people in a realistically described place and time. But it is also innovative in that it introduces elements of fantasy and mystery not normally present in the English novel. In this sense Hilton's novel is *original* for it not only places the story in an unusual setting — Tibet — but it also contains an underlying philosophical dimension and a layer of fantasy which place it above the commonplace. Moreover the novel ends on a note of uncertainty.

There is no doubt that Hilton attached much importance to the notion that a novel should tell a story. He wrote later:

> I confess I have a weakness for a novel that tells a story. It can do lots of other things besides, and its scenes can be laid in Tennessee or Timbuktu or Tibet; but a story, please, a story.[1]

Lost Horizon is certainly absorbing; for it tells an exciting tale which ensures that the reader will want to keep on turning the pages. At the same time it is clearly much more than a narrative of adventure in the vein of

Rider Haggard's *She*. It is designed not only to entertain but to stimulate thought. Seen in this light it can be said to mark a new departure.

It is also a new departure in the sense that the old order of literary "giants" was coming to an end. Thomas Hardy died in 1928, Arnold Bennett in 1931 and John Galsworthy in 1933. These luminaries were being replaced by a new generation of younger writers, some of whom had fresh and original things to say. Aldous Huxley's *Brave New World* (1932), a satire on material progress at the expense of the human spirit, echoed a widely held view that science and technology per se were no panacea for human ills.

It is significant that H.G. Wells's *The Shape of Things to Come* appeared in the same month and the same year as *Lost Horizon*. Both novels warn of the imminent danger of world war, but whereas Wells depicts a scenario of world conflict followed by reconstruction engineered by a technological elite, Hilton places his emphasis on "the things of that inner mind in which he lived increasingly, away from the fret of the world" (199). Hilton's concept is much more one of *preservation*— of garnering a treasure house of books, art, music and culture and saving them from destruction. Both books offered a timely parable on the theme of war and peace, but *Lost Horizon* held more appeal for those who valued contemplation and quietness in an increasingly strident world.

Lost Horizon caught the mood of the moment by seeming to offer hope and the promise of harmony and peace at a time of widespread unrest, conflict and violence.

During the years preceding its publication there had been a spate of books on the theme of disenchantment with war. These had included Gristwood's *The Somme* (1928), Erich Remarque's *All Quiet on the Western Front* (1929), R.C. Sherriff's *Journeys End* (1929) and Siegfried Sassoon's *Memoirs of an Infantry Officer* (1930).

There was a yearning at the time for novels and plays which offered a respite from war, anger and violence. It was not simply that the public yearned for the kind of entertainment which is disparagingly labeled "escapist," though it is true that the musical *The Cooptimists* appeared in 1929, Chaplin's *City Lights* in 1931 and the blockbuster film *King Kong* in 1933. It was rather more than that: a reaction from the intense patriotism of the war years and a recognition that the war had not achieved the freedom from strife for which people longed. This is the significance of the frequent references to 1914–1918 in *Lost Horizon* and to the High Lama's comment:

> But there is, I admit, an odd quality in you that I have never met in any of our visitors hitherto. It is not quite cynicism, still less bitterness; perhaps it is partly disillusionment, but it is also a clarity of mind that I should not have expected in anyone younger than — say, a century or so. It is, if I had to put a single word to it, passionlessness [156].

Conway then explains that he had used up his passions and energies during the war years and that since then his one desire is to be left alone: he has come to value peace and quietness above all things. *Lost Horizon* perfectly expresses this mood of disenchantment. In this sense the novel is a wish fulfillment since it embodies a widespread longing for peace and harmony.

The Social Background

The Wall Street crash in October 1929 (the collapse of the U.S. Stock Exchange) precipitated a world economic crisis leading to widespread depression and unemployment. The crash was followed by the cessation of U.S. loans to Europe, and this in turn had a "knock on" effect throughout the Western world. By 1932 unemployment in the U.S. had risen to 13.7 million, in Britain to 2.8 million and in Germany, to 5.6 million. It was a time of unrest, poverty and anger. In Britain hunger marches by the unemployed expressed the frustration and powerlessness of the dispossessed.

At the same time there were grounds for hope. In November 1932 Franklin Roosevelt won the presidential election by a landslide and in his inaugural address the following year launched the New Deal, boldly asserting that "the only thing we have to fear is fear itself." The New Deal was a brave attempt to reduce unemployment through a program of public works, providing credit at low interest, extensive house building, new rights for workers and a social insurance scheme. Through these measures unemployment in the U.S. was steadily reduced from 17 million to 7 million.

Here again *Lost Horizon* caught the public mood. By holding out the promise of a better future and a "promised land" of peace and happiness — at a time when many had no work and prospects seemed bleak — it expressed the basic human desire for a society governed by wisdom and enlightenment instead of discord. Of the millions who read it many would have their own personal vision of Shangri-La: a world without poverty and where people were motivated by nobler aspirations than simply trying to make ends meet.

By its implied criticism of the existing social order *Lost Horizon* offered an attractive vision of an alternative society. Barnard, for example, is a financier who asserts that "high finance is mostly a lot of bunk," Conway is totally disillusioned with many aspects of conventional society, and Chang points out many defects in Western civilization. Simply by offering an alternative blueprint the novel provided a channel for its readers hopes and dreams.

War Clouds

Throughout the time Hilton was researching and writing *Lost Horizon* war clouds were gathering ominously. In 1932 Japan invaded China and occupied Shanghai. In the same year Germany left the Geneva Disarmament Conference and the British Union of Fascists was formed. In January 1933 Hitler became chancellor of Germany, swiftly followed by the persecution of Jews, the suspension of civil liberties and the end of freedom of the press. Also in 1933 Japan decided to leave the League of Nations; there was a rising of anarchists in Spain; and Germany too walked out of the League. It was a time of widespread unrest and violence, an awareness that civilised values were breaking down as Nazism, Fascism and anarchism were on the ascendant.

The League of Nations, which had been launched with such high expectations in 1920, was increasingly impotent. Germany, Italy and Japan ignored their responsibilities; the United States declined to join; and Russia was ostracized by most other nations. In the face of aggression the League could only respond with economic sanctions, and even these were only half-heartedly applied. The failure of the League was becoming more and more apparent as the world edged towards war.

When the High Lama in *Lost Horizon* foresees the coming of war he speaks eloquently of the trampling of beauty and culture:

> He foresaw a time when men, exultant in the technique of homicide, would rage so hotly over the world that every precious thing would be in danger, every book and picture and harmony, every treasure garnered through two millenniums, the small, the delicate, the defenceless, all would be lost [158].

In anticipating so clearly the destructive effects of war Hilton gave a frighteningly accurate vision of what was to come. Already in the novel there are references to bombing raids (the Japanese attacks on China), torture (by revolutionaries in Afghanistan), and indiscriminate violence and carnage. In warning so eloquently of the impact of war the novel offers a timely forecast of what was in store only six years later.

Lost Horizon is a product of its time in the sense that its hero, Conway, is a man who has fought in the world war of 1914–1918 and can never forget his experiences. When the High Lama tells Conway he has never met his like before Conway replies that his own generation has passed through a unique and traumatic trial. It is because he has personally witnessed the horrors of war that he dreads the impact of another and longs so passionately for the peace and freedom from stress offered by Shangri-La. Hilton himself was just too young to have served in the war (though as a schoolboy he was aware of the weekly casualty lists announcing the deaths of his friends) but was fully aware that those who *had* served had undergone an experience never to be forgotten. For a generation of readers *Lost Horizon* was a pivotal book because it expressed a widely felt disenchantment with war and at the same time embodies their fears for the future.

The nuclear age can be said to have begun in 1932 when the British physicist John Cockcroft and the Irish physicist Ernest Walton succeeded in splitting the nucleus of an atom for the first time. Other researchers such as Robert Oppenheimer and Leo Szilard were quick to perceive the military implications of nuclear fission, but it was the pioneering work of Cockcroft in the early 1930s which ushered in the nuclear age.

How prophetic the words of the High Lama seem in the light of this:

> He saw the nations strengthening, not in wisdom, but in vulgar passions and the will to destroy; he saw their machine power multiplying until a single weaponed man might have matched a whole army of the Grand Monarque [157].

The fact that nuclear fission became a reality at the very time that *Lost Horizon* was conceived gives an added piquancy to this statement. Part of the background to the novel's conception was an alarming growth in the destructive power of weapons, and in the range of military technology on land, sea and air. In theory the League of Nations and the Kellogg Pact (which outlawed war as a means of settling disputes) made war *less* likely, but the reality is that the nations of Europe were arming and arming fast.

Aviation

Since much of the plot of *Lost Horizon* hinges on an epic airplane flight it is worth noting that during the years preceding its publication there were spectacular advances in aviation technology. In 1927 Charles Lindbergh flew from New York to Paris in 37 hours, an amazing achievement for its time. 1928 saw the first east-west transatlantic flights, in 1929 Richard Byrd flew over the South Pole, in 1930 Amy Johnson flew alone from London to Australia, in 1932 Codos flew from Paris to Hanoi and in 1933 Wiley Post flew round the world in 7 days and 18 hours. In that same year the Houston Expedition flew over Mount Everest. When one reflects that powered flight was not achieved until 1903 — thanks to the pioneering work of Orville and Wilbur Wright — the amount of progress attained in just 30 years is truly astonishing. Throughout those three decades there were substantial improvements in aircraft design, range, performance and durability.

It is significant that the opening scene of the novel is set at Tempel-hof airport, Berlin, for the German airline Lufthansa was one of the leaders in aviation advancement. In 1929 Lufthansa inaugurated the first postal service between Berlin and London, and in 1930 the airline opened the first regular service on the Vienna-Budapest-Belgrade-Sofia-Istanbul route. In April 1931 scheduled passenger services across the Alps commenced (hitherto felt to be an extremely hazardous undertaking) thanks to the three-engined Junkers 52, which brought a new standard of safety and punctuality to the Alpine route. Because of the sturdy construction and reliability of the Junkers 52 the plane soon established itself as the backbone of the airline, and it was widely used not only in Europe but also in South America and the Far East. These developments were paralleled by advances in Asia. In 1928 a Lufthansa machine flew from Berlin to Siberia: a journey of 8,000 miles in 76 hours, while in 1929 the Graf Zeppelin airship traveled from Friedrichshafen across the Far East to America, carrying 20 passengers. In 1930 another machine flew from Berlin to Baghdad to test the feasibility of a mail route via Istanbul to Asia Minor.

In May 1931 a regular airmail service between Berlin and Shanghai commenced (the service took seven to eight days, a gain of five to six days over the railway), and in the following year a regular route between Shanghai and the Russo-Chinese frontier began operations. In 1933 flight across the menacing Gobi desert in Mongolia was successfully attempted.

Lost Horizon postulates a plane journey between Baskul (Kabul) and the Kunlun mountains in Tibet: a distance of 900 miles flying at a high altitude. Would such a journey have been technically possible in 1931?

Hilton had certainly done his homework on this matter for in 1931 there were numerous aircraft which could have made such a journey including the Douglas Cloudster, the Lockheed Vega and the Curtiss Condor. It seems appropriate that in 1943 Hilton was invited to compère the series of radio plays sponsored by the Lockheed Company on the CBS station. In announcing the news in their journal the company stated, "It is with pride that Lockheed and Vega announce the acquisition of the services of the noted author."[2]

Tibet

It is difficult for us today to realize how remote Tibet was in the early years of the 20th century. We live in an age of instant communication, swift air travel, and an increasingly global community. But in the 1930s Tibet was almost unknown to readers in the Western world. The British explorer Francis Younghusband had succeeded in reaching Lhasa in 1904 but after his brief exploration Tibet had retreated once again into a shroud of mystery. A medieval theocracy surrounded by impenetrable mountain ranges, it was regarded as a lost world.

Younghusband — soldier, diplomat, explorer and geographer — had traveled widely in India and China and had been instrumental in opening up Tibet to the West. As president of the Royal Geographical Society from 1919 to 1922 Younghusband became the first chairman of the Mount Everest Committee, sponsoring the first three expeditions, in 1921, 1922 and 1924, in all of which Mallory participated (Mallory lost his life during the 1924 attempt). Younghusband enjoyed a high profile right up to his death in 1942. His obituary in the *New York Times* surmised, "If, as James Hilton strongly suggests in *Lost Horizon* Shangri-La is somewhere in Tibet rather than merely somewhere, anywhere ... then Sir Francis Younghusband probably came closer than anyone else to being Conway."[3]

When Hilton was asked why he chose to write about such a remote area he replied: "Obscure places and people have a great attraction for me and Tibet is one of the few places on earth that is still comparatively inaccessible."[4] The irony is that Hilton himself had never visited Tibet. Instead he had immersed himself in books about the country, and in particular had studied descriptions of Tibet written by the American explorer Joseph Rock, who had traveled widely in the country in the 1920s and 1930s. It was Rock's accounts in the *National Geographic Magazine*, with their vivid descriptions of lofty mountain ranges, windswept plateaus, and hidden valleys, which inspired Hilton to set his novel in this inhospitable terrain. It is highly probable that another of his sources was Younghusband's book *The Heart of a Continent* (1897), an account of the discovery of the route from Kashgar into India via the Mustagh Pass. The description of remote mountain passes in the Karakorums may well have inspired Hilton. We know that he spent many hours in the Reading Room of the British Museum studying descriptions of travel in Tibet. He wrote later, "I remember hours in libraries reading tales and legends of the great missionary travellers who explored all central Asia centuries ago."[5]

Long after the publication of *Lost Horizon* Tibet continued to be largely unknown. Heinrich Harrer's book *Seven Years in Tibet,* which includes fascinating descriptions of the country and its people in the 1940s, was not published until 1953. Tibet has, of course, been under Chinese occupation since 1950 but despite this vast tracts of the country are still mountainous and only nominally under Chinese rule. The Kunlun Mountains, where Hilton located Shangri-La, remain to this day largely unexplored. It is a vast mountain range containing peaks almost as high as Everest.

By the 1930s most of the unexplored regions of the world had been conquered. Central Africa had been an enigma for centuries (as late as 1860 maps showed the interior of the continent as a vast empty space) and parts of South America remained little known until the early twentieth century. For this reason novels such as Rider Haggard's *King Solomon's Mines* (1885) and Conan-Doyle's *The Lost World* (1912) had a wide appeal for contemporary readers: vivid descriptions of unknown lands held an irresistible fascination.

When an interviewer asked Hilton whether his descriptions of Tibet were wholly imaginary he replied:

> No; there is a large amount of reading behind them. The mountain of Karakal is imaginary — I don't suppose there is so lovely a mountain anywhere and it would be difficult to find in Tibet a lamasery as clean as Shangri-La, but much of what I have written about it is true. There is plenty of evidence, for instance, to support the ideas I have introduced of longevity and telepathy.[6]

Hilton also drew on the ancient Buddhist legend of Shambala, the idea of a sacred landscape hidden in the remote fastnesses of Tibet. There is no doubt that the concept of a lost paradise, known only to a select few, holds a powerful appeal to the imagination. The fact that Shambala has never been found and yet the legend persists simply adds to the story's appeal. The notion of a strange kingdom hidden in an elusive land finds a place in many literatures.

In a perceptive essay, "Aspects of Fantasy in Literary Myths about Lost Civilizations," Samuel Vasbinder has commented:

> Britain is rich in stories of strange castles and lost kingdoms.... Sir John Mandeville in his *Travels* records tales of far distant Cathay and the fabled land of Prester John. In this tradition also is More's *Utopia,* which depicts people living in the uttermost parts of the earth, a tale that contributed ideas to the more modern *Lost Horizon* by Hilton and *The Island* by Huxley. It is clear that man's fascination with strange places and forgotten peoples of the earth has exercised its charm for centuries.[7]

For these reasons Hilton's novel describing an idyllic civilization hidden in a lost Tibetan valley was considered deeply attractive. *Lost Horizon* vividly conveys a sense of remoteness, of a secluded valley tucked away behind impenetrable mountain peaks. Herein lies its appeal. In the end every reader loves a mystery.

8

Narrative Art

It is important to remember that before embarking on *Lost Horizon* Hilton had had a long apprenticeship in the craft of writing fiction. His first novel, *Catherine Herself,* was begun when he was only 17. This was followed by a further nine novels before the writing of his most famous story. In addition to writing fiction he was also a prolific journalist and critic, contributing articles and book reviews to a number of leading journals and newspapers. He had thus been writing for fifteen years before commencing work on *Lost Horizon* and throughout that time was gaining valuable experience in the art of the storyteller. The novel is clearly the work of an accomplished writer who knows how to hold the attention of the reader.

An examination of Hilton's original manuscript reveals that the novel was written and revised with great care. The typewritten draft is heavily revised in ink, with sentences and in some cases entire paragraphs rewritten or interpolated. The opening words, for example, were originally, "It was getting late." This was altered to, "The coffee had gone cold," and then altered again to the more familiar, "Cigars had burned low." Throughout Hilton was clearly at pains to achieve a dreamlike atmosphere, a haunting impression of a memorable experience recalled at leisure by a gifted raconteur. All the surviving manuscripts of his novels indicate that they were composed with meticulous care, and *Lost Horizon* especially so. When the manuscript came up for sale in 1949 it was described in the auctioneer's catalogue in these terms:

The alterations and revisions are unusually heavy, the majority of the leaves being re-written or modified, the alterations in words and phrases often being changed two or three times before a satisfactory effect was attained.[1]

The author sought throughout to attain a certain mood: one of mellow contemplation, as if a half-forgotten experience is recollected with mingled yearning and regret. A further example is the following sentence from Chapter 7:

Perrault, at any rate, did not then realize it. He was far too old and happy. His followers were devoted even when they forgot his teaching, while the people of the valley held him in such reverent affection that he forgave with ever-increasing ease their lapse into former customs [137].

The original draft reads:

For suddenly, putting aside all doubts he might have had, Perrault had come to be very happy at Shangri-La; despite an inclination to former customs the monks were all devoted to him, while the valley people revered him more than ever, though they also were guilty of forgetfulness rather than disobedience.

Again the final version is more fluent and felicitous, employing a smaller number of words to achieve the desired effect.

The care with which the novel was composed suggests that Hilton sensed he had hit upon a refreshing and original theme and was determined to do his utmost to achieve memorable and distinguished prose.

Lost Horizon has not been out of print since its original publication in Britain and the United States in 1933, and it continues to be available in both hardback and paperback editions. In contrast, many novels which were immensely popular in the 1930s have since faded into oblivion — including best selling titles by such authors as Warwick Deeping, Howard Spring, Arthur Hutchinson and Michael Arlen.[2] Clearly *Lost Horizon* possesses literary and imaginative qualities which have ensured its survival into a new century. In this chapter we will talk a closer look at some of the literary techniques employed by Hilton including his style and use of language, his characterization, the structure of the novel and the narrative voice.

The Narrative Voice

In *Lost Horizon* Hilton follows the long established device of enclosing the narrative within a "frame." The central narrative, Chapters 1–11, describing Conway's journey to Shangri-La and his experiences there, are based on Conway's account but have been written down by Rutherford, a professional novelist. These chapters are enclosed within a Prologue and Epilogue told by an unnamed narrator. All we know of him is that he is a neurologist, that he was at school with Conway and is a friend of Rutherford's. Rutherford's story is filtered through the consciousness of the unnamed narrator, and Conway's story in turn is filtered through the consciousness of Rutherford. The result of this is to give a *distancing* effect to the narrative. It would have been possible for Hilton to have told the story in the first person with Conway as the narrator. Conway would then have been the "I" telling the story. Hilton wisely decided not to do this. Instead he chose to place the story "at one remove" by having it retold by Rutherford, a writer who is inclined to be skeptical of Conway's story but is intrigued by it. The fact that both Rutherford and the neurologist knew Conway and admired him for his charisma and charm adds to the story's conviction. At the same time the detachment of the neurologist (we know little about him and do not even know his name) means that he is not directly involved in the story and can therefore view it dispassionately. If the Prologue and Epilogue were narrated by one of the principal characters we would regard him as a subjective witness. As it is we are inclined to suspend disbelief precisely because the opening and closing sections are told in such a calm and matter-of-fact tone.

The Prologue serves an additional function as well as acting as a frame. Because the Prologue is rooted firmly in the world of fact these opening pages help to establish the veracity of Conway's narrative. The scene is set at a real location — Tempelhof airport in Berlin — at a dinner attended by four people, three of whom are named. They discuss the hijacking of a plane and are told the month and year when this event took place: May 1931. They talk about a mutual acquaintance, an Englishman named Conway, and Rutherford, one of the guests at the dinner, states that he attended the same school. The conversation then turns to Conway's achievements at Oxford University and his service during the First World War when he was awarded a D.S.O. All these apparent facts create an atmosphere of reality which paves the way for the story that follows. By the time the reader turns to the first sentence of Chapter 1 and learns the precise date of the beginning of Conway's adventures we are fully prepared to believe all that we are told.

In choosing to tell his story in this way Hilton is following in an honorable tradition, that of the "tale within a tale."

The Reader and the Text

Reading a work of fiction for the second or third time is a different experience from a first reading. This is particularly true of *Lost Horizon,* which is a comparatively short novel that engages the attention of the reader from the first page. In a first reading one's entire attention is on the story itself: what happens next? In subsequent readings details are noticed which were not apparent before, the language and style employed by the writer is more noticeable, there is a greater appreciation of literary techniques. Why, for example, has the novelist decided to tell his story in this particular way? Is there a narrative voice with a particular point of view? And above all, how has the writer achieved the distinctive atmosphere of this novel? Many readers of *Lost Horizon* testify that the book has a haunting quality and that some of the scenes depicted in the story remain indelibly in the mind. One thinks, for example, of the graphic description of the journey across the mountain ranges to Tibet, the encounter with Chang in his hooded chair, the first sight of Shangri-La, the conversations with the High Lama, Conway's succession to the leadership of the community, his decision to leave Shangri-La and his departure into the outside world. Each of these scenes is described with extraordinary vividness, as if Hilton himself has witnessed them. During Conway's first meeting with the High

Lama Hilton states "it appeared that the High Lama had been translating, with fluency, out of a remote and private dream." The reader has precisely this feeling when studying *Lost Horizon*. It is above all an *absorbing* novel, written fluently and vividly in prose of compelling power. In common with Wells's *The Time Machine,* Stevenson's *Treasure Island* and du Maurier's *Rebecca* it is one of those novels which, once read, is never forgotten.

Lost Horizon does not simply engage the reader intellectually but also does so emotionally. I know of no other novel which leaves the reader with such a haunting sense of loss. When Conway regains his memory and we are told that his face had stiffened "into what I can only describe as an expression of overwhelming sadness" we do not know at that stage why he is so unhappy, but by the time we have read his story we fully share his regret. Conway is a man consumed with regret for the world he has lost (another reason why the title of the novel is so apt). It is difficult to read the book without sharing this sense of yearning. Long after we have finished reading it the feeling of loss remains in the mind, a feeling that can only be satiated by reading the novel again and absorbing oneself in its special atmosphere. *Lost Horizon* is one of those novels which have attracted a loyal following of devotees, readers who return to it at frequent intervals because they find the book so appealing. How have these effects been achieved?

It is partly a matter of *language*. Hilton was a skilled practitioner who had developed a smooth and accomplished prose style capable of expressing a wide range of feelings. An interesting example of this occurs in the moments leading up to Conway's first encounter with the High Lama, Father Perrault. The language is carefully chosen to achieve an atmosphere of suspense:

> "The High Lama," whispered Chang, "will receive you alone."
> Having opened the door for Conway's entrance, he closed it afterwards so silently that his own departure was almost imperceptible. Conway stood hesitant, breathing an atmosphere that was not only sultry, but full of dusk, so that it was several seconds before he could accustom his eyes to the gloom. Then he slowly built up an impression of a dark-curtained low-roofed apartment, simply furnished with table and chairs. On one of these sat a small, pale, and wrinkled person, motionlessly shadowed, and yielding an effect as

of some fading, antique portrait in chiaroscuro. If there were such
a thing as presence divorced from actuality, here it was, adorned
with a classic dignity that was more an emanation than an attrib-
ute. Conway was curious about his own intense perception of all
this, and wondered if it were dependable or merely his reaction to
the rich crepuscular warmth; he felt dizzy under the gaze of those
ancient eyes, took a few forward paces, and then halted. The occu-
pant of the chair grew now less vague in outline, but scarcely more
corporeal; he was a little old man in Chinese dress, its folds and
flounces loose against a flat, emaciated frame. "You are Mr. Conway?" he whispered in excellent English.
   The voice was pleasantly soothing, and touched with a very gentle melancholy that fell upon Conway with strange beatitude
[129–130].

We note first the reiteration of words suggestive of darkness: dusk,
gloom, dark-curtained, shadowed. This is followed by a number of expres-
sions designed to convey an impression of great age: fading, antique,
ancient, melancholy, emaciated. Skillfully Hilton creates an aura of anticipation — both Conway himself and the reader are aware of a sense of
expectation: "presence divorced from actuality," "adorned with a classic
dignity," "his own intense perception," "with a strange beatitude." The
entire passage creates an atmosphere of suspense — the silent closing of the
door, the shadowed room, the sultry atmosphere, the air of mystery. The
reader shares with Conway his sense that he is on the brink of revelation.
This is heightened by the fact that he feels dizzy, he is unaccustomed to
the intense heat, he is unsure what to expect and is filled with a vague
sense of uneasiness. Above all he is conscious that he is in the presence of
a venerable and revered figure.
   A further example occurs immediately following the death of the
High Lama. Conway stumbles from the apartment, uncertain how to sum-
mon help. It is late at night and he is alone:

He stood uncertainly on the threshold of the dark corridor;
through a window he could see that the sky was clear, though the
mountains still blazed in lightning like a silver fresco. And then, in
the midst of the still encompassing dream, he felt himself master of
Shangri-La. These were his beloved things, all around him, the
things of that inner mind in which he lived increasingly, away from
the fret of the world. His eyes strayed into the shadows and were

caught by golden pinpoints sparkling in rich, undulating lacquers; and the scent of tuberose, so faint that it expired on the very brink of sensation, lured him from room to room. [199–200].

In this passage the reader has a sense of Conway's innermost feelings on learning of his succession: "These were his beloved things, all around him, the things of that inner mind in which he lived." He feels himself to be "master of Shangri-La." But Hilton strengthens this effect by the addition of circumstantial details which fix the scene in the imagination: the thunderstorm, shadows, sparkling pinpoints of light, the scent of tuberose. These details heighten the feeling of drama. Conway is poised at a turning point in the story, elevated to the headship of Shangri-La but faced with the imminent decision of whether to leave or remain. The words, "He stood uncertainly on the threshold of the dark corridor" perfectly express his dilemma, while the addition of the phrase, "in the midst of the still encompassing dream" underlines the dream-like, haunting quality which permeates the story.

It is also a matter of *mood*. Throughout the novel Hilton is trying to achieve a certain atmosphere. He himself clearly finds Shangri-La and its underlying philosophy deeply attractive and wishes his readers to share this feeling. Shangri-La is described in terms such as "superb," "exquisite," "dream-like," "elegant," "delicate," "fragile," "calm," "lovely." The reader is left with an indelible impression of a lost valley surrounded by impenetrable mountain ranges, a haven of peace and learning in an increasingly dangerous world.

Another technique employed by Hilton is that of *suspense*. Gradually a sense of anticipation is built up so that at any moment the reader is expecting a revelation:

The truth was the puzzle of Shangri-La and of his own arrival there was beginning to exercise over him a rather charming fascination [82].

He had heard enough to turn another key in the locked mystery, and it fitted so well that he wondered he had failed to supply it by his own deductions [103].

For what possible reason could four chance passengers in a British Government aeroplane be whisked away to these trans-Himalayan solitudes? [103].

101

> If the words of the Chinese meant anything, he was on the
> threshold of discovery; soon he would know whether his theory,
> still half formed, were less impossible than it appeared [128–129].

The moment of revelation — when Conway learns the truth about Shangri-La and that he and his companions are to remain there permanently — occurs two-thirds of the way through the novel. Until then both Conway and the reader are in doubt. The sense of anticipation culminates in his long conversation with the High Lama and the discovery that he alone is to be entrusted with the truth.

One of the reasons why this novel is so compellingly readable is that Hilton builds up a mood of anticipation which makes the book difficult to put down.

Language

When the novel was first published the critic Margaret Pope described it as "a book to handle with gratitude for an exquisite conception, exquisitely carried out."[3]

This may seem extravagant praise but a close reading of the novel reveals a highly felicitous use of language which adds greatly to the impact of the story upon the reader. The hidden lamasery of Shangri-La is described in elegant and attractive prose, so much so that some of the scenes and descriptive passages remain indelibly in the mind.

Consider, for example, the memorable passage in which Conway and his companions encounter the emissaries from Shangri-La for the first time:

> Part of Conway was always an onlooker, however active might be the rest. Just now, while waiting for the strangers to come nearer, he refused to be fussed into deciding what he might or mightn't do in any number of possible contingencies. And this was not bravery, or coolness, or any especially sublime confidence in his own power to make decisions on the spur of the moment. It was, if the worst view be taken, a form of indolence — an unwillingness to interrupt his mere spectator's interest in what was happening.

As the figures moved down the valley they revealed themselves to be a party of a dozen or more, carrying with them a hooded chair. In this, a little later, could be discerned a person robed in blue. Conway could not imagine where they were all going, but it certainly seemed providential, as Miss Brinklow had said, that such a detachment should chance to be passing just there and then. As soon as he was within hailing distance he left his own party and walked ahead, though not hurriedly, for he knew that Orientals enjoy the ritual of meeting and like to take their time over it. Halting when a few yards off, he bowed with due courtesy.

Much to his surprise the robed figure stepped from the chair, came forward with dignified deliberation, and held out his hand. Conway responded, and observed an old or elderly Chinese, grey-haired, clean-shaven, and rather pallidly decorative in a silk embroidered gown. He in his turn appeared to be submitting Conway to the same kind of ready reckoning. Then, in precise and perhaps too accurate English, he said: "I am from the lamasery of Shangri-La" [55–56].

The passage merits careful study as an illustration of Hilton's technique. The statement that "Part of Conway was always an onlooker, however active might be the rest" is a timely reminder of the divided nature of Conway's personality: he is both a man of action and a man of contemplation. However much he desires action and resolution he is content in situations of this kind to be an observer: to be a passive witness of events and not seek to shape them. In any case he is well aware that in their present predicament the survivors of the plane crash have little alternative but to accept their fate.

The neutral, unemotional language of the passage emphasizes Conway's passivity: "they revealed themselves to be," "could be discerned," "should chance to be passing," "though not hurriedly," "he bowed with due courtesy." The tone suggests a tableau which Hilton wishes to fix indelibly in the imagination. It is not only Conway who is an onlooker but the reader also — it is as if we are looking over Conway's shoulder and seeing what he sees. It is not simply Conway who is astonished at meeting the dignified Chinese in the hooded chair but the reader also. The language of the entire passage is designed to imprint the scene firmly on the mind.

This encounter with Chang and the Tibetans is one of the famous "set pieces" of the novel, made even more memorable from the numerous film and radio adaptations of the story. As we read the passage we see the entire tableau before us: the sloping valley, the hooded chair, the enigmatic figure robed in blue, the robed figure stepping from the chair, the formal greeting. The fact of encountering human beings in such a remote spot is astonishing enough: what is even more remarkable is the dignified formality of the meeting and the fact that the strange figure in an embroidered gown speaks perfect English.

The language of the paragraph is deceptively simple and is greatly helped by the third person method of narration Hilton has chosen to adopt. Conway is not the narrator, yet he remains the focal point of the encounter. It is from *his* perspective that we observe the scene. It is Conway who refuses to be perturbed, who speculates on where the Tibetans might be going, and who knows that the Orientals enjoy the ritual of meeting. Had the scene been told in the first person the dispassionate tone Hilton is at pains to achieve would inevitably have been lost. At this point in the story Hilton is anxious that his readers should not prejudge Shangri-La and its emissaries: he wishes events simply to unfold, and to allow the reader to form his own conclusions. The unemotional language is calculated to achieve this. The tone is not at all subjective, but simply matter-of-fact. The word "spectator" is interesting in this connection. The apparent blandness of the vocabulary obscures the fact that it is extraordinarily effective.

Because the story is not told in the first person it is easy to assume from this paragraph that Hilton is "not present": the reader is not aware of an authorial presence. Yet the author is there all the time, guiding and shaping. It is the author who creates the perspective from which we view the scene, and it is he who determines the sequence of events and he who sets the *tone*. Notice the absence of emotive or subjective language. The entire incident is described in simple, economical prose.

This example is one of many which could be chosen to illustrate Hilton's skill as a writer. His style is rarely "flowery" or pretentious, but fluent, direct and yet impressive. Whether he is describing the inhospitable terrain of the Tibetan mountains, the soothing calm of Shangri-La, the peaceful valley of Blue Moon or the death of the High Lama he succeeds in depicting the scene in memorable prose that is a pleasure to read. A reading group which had studied *Lost Horizon* commented: "We are enchanted by the book; the writing is exquisite, and a sense of timelessness pervades it."[4]

The conversations between the High Lama and Conway are particularly rich in fine writing and will repay careful study as illustrations of Hilton's literary technique. At one point the High Lama draws attention to his own eloquence, saying: "Forgive my eloquence — I belong to an age and a nation that never considered it bad form to be articulate" [154].

The final conversation between the two men, in which the heritage of Shangri-La is bequeathed to Conway, contains many memorable passages. If some of these passages are recast in the form of verse their literary quality at once becomes apparent:

> It is not an arduous task that I bequeath
> for our order knows only silken bonds.
> To be gentle and patient
> To care for the riches of the mind
> To preside in wisdom and secrecy
> while the storm rages without...
>
> You will conserve the fragrance
>   of our history
> and add to it the touch of your own mind.
> You will welcome the stranger
> and teach him the rule of age and wisdom...
>
> I see, at a great distance,
> a new world stirring in the ruins
> stirring clumsily but in hopefulness
> seeking its lost and legendary treasures.
>
> And they will all be here...
> hidden behind the mountains,
> preserved as by miracle
> for a new Renaissance [197–199].

It is clear that this is a carefully executed piece of writing, a reminder of the fact that for Hilton language is an instrument for both shaping a narrative and communicating a mood, an atmosphere.

The reader has an inescapable sense of the High Lama as a *person*, a character who is not simply a cerebral figure but a man who belongs to an age when thoughts were expressed in fluent and enduring terms.

This is one example which is typical of many in which the author interweaves the text with a web of connotative prose which both heightens and transforms the narrative. Where Hilton's novels are unsuccessful — as in *Morning Journey*, for example — it is precisely because this literary and poetic quality is absent. In his finest work he is interweaving the narrative with a tracery which functions both as an imaginative and didactic frame.

The Journey

Hilton skillfully creates a mood of anticipation and suspense throughout the early chapters by the continual use of language associated with a *journey*. Time and again we are reminded that the four passengers are embarked on a journey to an unknown destination: "the plane soared aloft," "the plane rose high into the hazy vapors," "the flight proceeded," "meanwhile the plane, on that stupendous stage, was droning over an abyss." The Pocket Books edition runs to 230 pages, but it is not until page 66 that the reader is given his first glimpse of Shangri-La. Throughout the first 66 pages Hilton carefully builds up the suspense and prepares the reader for an emotional and intellectual experience. *Lost Horizon* is a deeply thought-provoking work but it is also an exciting adventure story. The sense of embarking on a journey comes to a conclusive end with the arrival at Shangri-La:

> To Conway, seeing it first, it might have been a vision fluttering out of that solitary rhythm in which lack of oxygen had encompassed all his faculties. It was, indeed, a strange and almost incredible sight. A group of colored pavilions clung to the mountainside with none of the grim deliberation of a Rhineland castle, but rather with the chance delicacy of flower-petals impaled upon a crag. It was superb and exquisite....
> Conway experienced, as he gazed, a slight tightening of apprehension; Mallinson's misgivings were not, perhaps, to be wholly disregarded. But the feeling was only momentary, and soon merged in the deeper sensation, half mystical, half visual, of having reached at last some place that was an end, a finality [66–67].

Through the first three chapters a sense of *movement* has been created: there is an awareness that we are traveling towards an unknown destination. The plane journey is saturated with such words as "fearsome," "raw," "monstrous," "distant," "inaccessible," "icy," "remote." The reader shares with the four passengers their unease that they are being taken against their will to a wholly unexplored and mysterious region — for a reason that is still unexplained. Only the words "having reached at last some place that was an end, a finality" prepare us for the idea that at last journey's end has been reached.

The Four Passengers

One of the most interesting aspects of the story is the relationship and interplay between the four characters who are transported to Shangri-La. At an early stage in the narrative Conway reflects that "the party might have been far less fortunately constituted," though indeed the four are very different. Conway himself is calm, philosophical, detached; Mallinson is young, ardent and impetuous; Barnard is pragmatic, unscrupulous and worldly; and Miss Brinklow is prim, conventional and rather comical in her narrow-mindedness.

Because the characters are temperamentally so diverse they each see Shangri-La in a different light. Conway is increasingly attracted toward the lamasery since he secretly hankers after a life of learning. To Mallinson on the other hand the lamasery is a *prison* from which he is anxious to escape. Barnard as a practical businessman is intrigued by the lamasery's source of income and offers to assist in improving its output of gold. To Miss Brinklow her sojourn at Shangri-La is a heaven-sent opportunity to convert the lamas to her own beliefs. An illustration of this is the scene in Chapter 5 when Chang offers to give the party a guided tour of the lamasery buildings. Conway submits to "a rich and growing enchantment" when he sees the priceless works of art and extensive library; Mallinson is willfully incurious and peeved that he cannot find a map showing their location; Barnard is baffled by the transport problem and wants to know how furniture and musical instruments are brought across the mountains; Miss Brinklow demands to know how the lamas occupy their time:

> "What do the lamas do?" she continued.
> "They devote themselves, madam, to contemplation and to the pursuit of wisdom."
> "But that isn't *doing* anything."
> "Then, madam, they do nothing."
> "I thought as much." She found occasion to sum up. "Well, Mr. Chang, it's a pleasure being shown all these things, I'm sure, but you won't convince me that a place like this does any real good. I prefer something more practical."
> "Perhaps you would like to take tea?" [96].

This humorous exchange (though of course Miss Brinklow does not see the joke) neatly encapsulates opposing attitudes of mind. Chang is an embodiment of the philosophy of Shangri-La: he is cautious, scholarly, tolerant and subtle. Miss Brinklow sees life in simple black-and-white terms: she and she alone is right and all other beliefs are wrong.

Hugh Conway is a typical Hilton hero in that he lives largely in the world of the mind. At an early stage in the narrative we are told that "What most observers failed to perceive in him was something quite bafflingly simple — a love of quietness, contemplation, and being alone" [36]. In this he has much in common with the central characters of other Hilton novels such as Charles Rainier in *Random Harvest* and Charles Anderson in *Time and Time Again.*[5] Conway is a man who outwardly could be regarded as a success — at the age of 37 he is a senior government official — yet it is evident that worldly success bores him and that he yearns for a fulfilling purpose in life. One of the most interesting aspects of *Lost Horizon* is the skilful manner in which Conway's personality is gradually unfolded. Slowly, by degrees, we learn more about him: that his heart is not really in his work, that he has been profoundly affected by his war experiences, that he is bored by protocol and looks back with regret to his life as an Oxford don.

An apt example of Hilton's technique is in Chapter One, where two processes are simultaneously at work. The substance of the first chapter is an account of the journey by plane from Baskul to an unknown destination. Gradually the passengers realize that the plane has been hijacked and each in his own way begins to respond to this alarming situation. But interwoven with this dramatic scenario is a slow unfolding of Conway's personality and temperament. Skillfully Hilton takes the reader inside Conway's mind, and for several paragraphs we share his innermost thoughts and feelings. The reader has been prepared for this by the frequent references to him in the Prologue: we are already aware that he is a remarkable and charismatic individual. As the story proceeds we see Conway becoming more and more attracted by Shangri-La and all that it represents. This is vividly conveyed in his account of his first meeting with the High Lama and the moment when he takes his leave:

> He was not perfectly aware of how at last he took his leave; he was in a dream from which he did not emerge till long afterwards. He remembered the night air icy after the heat of those upper rooms, and Chang's presence, a silent serenity, as they crossed the starlit courtyards together. Never had Shangri-La offered more concentrated loveliness to his eyes; the valley lay imagined over the edge of the cliff, and the image was of a deep unrippled pool that matched the peace of his own thoughts. For Conway had passed beyond astonishments. The long talk, with its varying phases, had left him empty of all save a satisfaction that was as much of the mind as of the emotions, and as much of the spirit as of either; even his doubts were now no longer harassing, but part of a subtle harmony. Chang did not speak, and neither did he. It was very late, and he was glad that all the others had gone to bed [159].

The language of this passage reinforces the dreamlike atmosphere Hilton is seeking to achieve: Conway "was in a dream," his thoughts are of peace, he is contented and silent. Chang's presence is described as "a silent serenity"; a phrase which perfectly expresses Conway's mood. Any conversation at this stage would have been in intrusion; he wishes simply to be left alone with his thoughts. The reference to the "concentrated loveliness" of Shangri-La reminds the reader of all that Conway finds appealing in this hidden community, while the phrase "the valley lay imagined over the edge of the cliff" contrasts the beauty of Shangri-La with the awesome precipice below. To Conway the image is of "a deep unrippled pool": at present he is undisturbed by the thought that all this may one day come to an end. Note also that his contentment is "as much of the mind as of the emotions." This phrase neatly balances the two sides of his personality.

Clearly Hilton is attracted by Conway; this is perhaps inevitable since Conway and Hilton have so much in common — they share a love of music, reading, quietness and mountaineering. It is the thoughtful, philosophical aspects of his personality which attract the High Lama so much. To Mallinson, on the other hand, these are not Conway's "true" nature but rather his abilities as a natural leader. The clash between these opposing attitudes is evident throughout the novel. From Mallinson's point of view Conway has wasted his time at Shangri-La — he has simply "mooned about as if nothing mattered." To Conway it is Mallinson who is impetuous and truculent, and he cannot understand why his young friend does not share his feeling of contentment.

Some critics have argued that the characters in *Lost Horizon* are one-dimensional. James Poling, for example, stated:

> *Lost Horizon* is in conception an extremely original novel. But the characters are intellectually, not emotionally, realized: more grey matter than red corpuscles has entered into their composition. And they have a tendency to run to type ... in so doing they frequently cease to be individuals and become, instead, mental concepts. And so the book is not completely convincing.[6]

It is arguable that there is some substance in this criticism as far as Mallinson, Barnard and Miss Brinklow are concerned. It is true that they tend to run to type and that in that sense their behavior in rather predictable. Mallinson is hasty and hot tempered, distrustful of Chang and eager to escape from Shangri-La at the earliest opportunity; Barnard is cynical and unrefined, disillusioned with material success yet with an eye on the main chance; Miss Brinklow is convinced she has been sent to Tibet for a purpose and disapproves of the lamasery because in her eyes it is lax and amoral.

Conway, however, is a more complex figure. Though he is clearly a man of intellect he is also capable of deep emotions. He is drawn toward the lamasery by "a deep spiritual emotion, as if Shangri-La were indeed a living essence, distilled from the magic of the ages and miraculously preserved against time and death" (170). He is strongly attracted by Lo-Tsen, the enigmatic Manchu girl who fascinates him by her apparent youthfulness and charm. He is awed by the regal presence of the High Lama and drawn increasingly toward that shrewd, benign intelligence. Above all he is enchanted by Shangri-La itself and all that it represents: "he liked the serene world that Shangri-La offered him, pacified rather than dominated by its single tremendous idea" (189). Conway is a man of many contradictions. When the situation demands it he can offer leadership and command; at the same time he can be at home in the world of books, music and ideas.

Several incidents in the novel neatly highlight the contrast between Conway's philosophical detachment and Mallinson's impetuosity. There is, for example, the episode during the plane journey when Mallinson urges a direct confrontation with the pilot (pp. 33–34). There could not be a sharper contrast between impulsiveness and impatience on the one hand and a preference for caution on the other. The younger man is all for the use of force whereas Conway instinctively favors calmness and patience. A second example is the scene in which Mallinson discovers Barnard's real identity (pp. 115–124). Again Mallinson, with his simple schoolboy code of honor, urges immediate exposure and denunciation. Conway, in total contrast, counsels caution and inactivity. Each of these incidents underlines the temperamental differences between the two men — Conway is typically English in his quietness, calmness, willingness to compromise and anxiety to avoid unpleasantness. Yet from Mallinson's perspective these qualities smack of indolence and slackness.

Conway stands out as a character precisely because he is presented "in the round." We not only see him as he sees himself but also as others see him. Of all the characters in *Lost Horizon* it is Conway who is the most "real" in the sense that he is a person who lives and breathes and feels.

Lo-Tsen

If the importance of a character is measured by the number of pages devoted to her then the Manchu girl Lo-Tsen would not normally be regarded as of major significance. Yet this enigmatic character plays a pivotal role in the novel. It is she to whom Conway is deeply attracted, it is she in turn who falls in love with Mallinson, and, crucially, it is she who arranges with the porters for her own and Mallinson's escape.

Lo-Tsen, though apparently a young girl, had arrived at the lamasery in 1884 when she was eighteen; she is therefore in reality 65 in 1931. Chang explains that she is of royal Manchu stock and had been betrothed to a prince of Turkestan. She was traveling to Kashgar to meet him when her party of escorts lost their way in the mountains. Lo-Tsen is to outward appearances a beautiful young woman, and she is an accomplished musician. Both Conway and Mallinson find her intriguing and long to find out more about her. What is she doing in a Tibetan lamasery? What does she really think? Is she happy? The words used to describe her are "finished," "miniature," "formal," "attractive," "statuesque," "elegant," "lovely" and "fragrant." Mallinson is attracted by her apparent youth and physical beauty, but for Conway she is the embodiment of both his emotional and intellectual desires:

> He was, and he knew it, very quietly in love with the little Manchu. His love demanded nothing, not even reply; it was a tribute of the mind, to which his senses added only a flavor. She stood for him as a symbol of all that was delicate and fragile; her stylized courtesies and the touch of her fingers on the keyboard yielded a completely satisfying intimacy.... And suddenly then he realized that Shangri-La and Lo-Tsen were quite perfect, and that he did not wish for more than to stir a faint and eventual response in all that stillness [178, 188].

It is interesting to note that throughout the novel Lo-Tsen does not speak. Her silence adds to the air of mystery surrounding her. When Chang reveals that he also had been in love with her when he was a young man this strengthens the reader's image of an alluring young woman and provides an additional bond between Chang and Conway.

It is arguable that the characters in *Lost Horizon* are open to criticism on the grounds that they exist mentally rather than emotionally. Lo-Tsen alters this perspective; Conway is forced to admit to himself that he is in love with her: "For years his passions had been like a nerve that the world jarred on; now at last the aching was soothed, and he could yield himself to love that was neither a torment nor a bore" [188].

This is not simply the conventional "love interest" that is a stock feature of so many Hollywood films. Lo-Tsen obliges Conway to come to terms with his deepest emotions, and forces Mallinson in turn to recognize her worth. It is for this reason that copies of the novel sometimes carry the phrase, "The haunting novel of love in Shangri-La" on the cover. Lo-Tsen is the catalyst who ultimately obliges Conway to leave Shangri-La, for she has fallen in love with Mallinson and he with her. It is Conway's recognition of this fact, and that Mallinson cannot live without her which is the turning point in the novel.

Lo-Tsen plays a central role in the narrative for it is she, alone of all the lamasery inhabitants, who engages Conway's innermost feelings. For the High Lama he feels admiration and respect, and for Chang he feels warm friendship, but it is the "little Manchu" who engages his deepest emotions. In providing Conway with companionship and solace Lo-Tsen evokes a response from him and thus provides the narrative with an emotional perspective it would otherwise lack. Without Lo-Tsen *Lost Horizon* would still be a gripping narrative but her presence brings a human touch which enhances the story and prevents it from being merely a cerebral account.

There is an additional sense in which Lo-Tsen is central to an understanding of the novel. There are frequent references to her enigmatic quality, to her unattainability. Chang emphasizes that "It has always been her way to spare her lovers the moment of satiety that goes with all absolute attainment" (187). At the end of the novel Conway pleads with Mallinson not to take her out of the valley, telling him that her beauty is "a fragile thing that can only live where fragile things are loved. Take it away from this valley and you will see it fade like an echo" (212). This last phrase — repeated word for word in the Frank Capra film — is a reminder that Lo-Tsen, in common with Weena in Wells' *The Time Machine* and Ayesha in Rider Haggard's *She*, is an Anima figure, the female shadow figure in the male psyche. She is the reassuring presence who beckons and consoles. It is precisely her unattainability which Conway finds so intriguing, the sense that he can never solve her mysteries or fully understand her. In fairy tales or in the symbolism of dreams the Anima figure is sometimes cut off by glass or ice, or she is enchanted or trapped in a castle. Lo-Tsen is a prisoner in a secluded valley from which she tries to escape; on leaving it she withers and dies, placing herself forever beyond Conway's reach. In this sense *Lost Horizon* can be seen as another variant on the classic theme of the unattainable goddess figure: a theme which haunts English literature from Arthurian legend to the present day. This is perfectly expressed in a passage when Conway imagines himself embracing her:

> As he passed by the lotus-pool at night he sometimes pictured her in his arms, but the sense of time washed over the vision, calming him to an infinite and tender reluctance [188–89].

Is this Conway's recognition that she will never be his? Indeed, "the sense of time washed over the vision" is a telling phrase, for it is indeed time which ultimately destroys her. Silent, inscrutable, mysterious, baffling: Lo-Tsen is one of Hilton's most haunting creations.

Imagery

The central image which dominates the novel is that of Karakal, the mountain overlooking the lost valley. It is first described in unforgettable terms:

> But it was to the head of the valley that his eyes were led irresistibly, for there, soaring into the gap, and magnificent in the full shimmer of moonlight, appeared what he took to be the loveliest mountain on earth. It was an almost perfect cone of snow, simple in outline as if a child had drawn it, and impossible to classify as to size, height, or nearness. It was so radiant, so serenely poised, that he wondered for a moment if it were real at all. Then, while he gazed, a tiny puff clouded the edge of the pyramid, giving life to the vision before the faint rumble of the avalanche confirmed it [50].

The language of this passage imprints the image on the mind of the reader: "magnificent," "loveliest," "perfect," "radiant," "serene." There is also a sense of unreality, as if the vision is not quite real. To Conway the mountain appears to be both solid and illusory, and he wonders momentarily if he is seeing a mirage.

In the language of dreams mountains symbolize the highest longings and aspirations of man. Mountains also symbolize obstacles which could be regarded as a challenge. In this sense Karakal is an apt metaphor for the dilemma confronting Conway. Emotionally he is drawn toward the life of the mind represented by Shangri-La, but intellectually he is aware that he has duties and responsibilities in the "real" world outside. This is made explicit a little later when he contemplates the mountain again:

> Framed in the pale triangle ahead, the mountain showed again, grey at first, then silver, then pink as the earliest sunrays caught the summit. In the lessening gloom the valley itself took shape, revealing a floor of rock and shingle sloping upwards. It was not a friendly picture, but to Conway, as he surveyed, there came a queer perception of fineness in it, of something that had no romantic appeal at all, but a steely, almost intellectual quality. The white pyramid in the distance compelled the mind's assent as passionlessly as a Euclidean theorem, and when at last the sun rose into a sky of deep delphinium-blue, he felt only a little less than comfortable again [52].

This passage is significant for several reasons. There is a deliberate contrast between "intellectual" and "romantic," the two sides of Conway's personality. On the one hand he is a man of action, a man who can provide leadership and decision when these qualities are required. But he is also a dreamer and romantic who admits that his heart has never been in his work and who secretly longs for a life of contemplation. Note also the reference to the "white pyramid," the mountain which is referred to again and again in the novel and which forms the background to so much of the action. The whiteness of the mountain is contrasted with the blueness of the sky: in psychological terms, white symbolizes the feminine aspects of Conway's personality and blue represents his yearning for contemplation and passivity. In this key paragraph, placed early in the story and even before his first sight of Shangri-La, is prefigured the central theme of the novel: the choice between the world of the mind and the world of practicality.

But as well as symbolizing aspiration the mountain also represents danger. When Karakal is referred to again it is described in terms which leave no doubt of its potential hazards:

> It might well be, Conway thought, the most terrifying mountain-scape in the world, and he imagined the immense stress of snow and glacier against which the rock functioned as a gigantic retaining wall. Some day, perhaps, the whole mountain would split, and a half of Karakal's icy splendor come toppling into the valley. He wondered if the slightness of the risk combined with its fearfulness might even be found agreeably stimulating [66].

Here the language is no longer the language of dreams but of acute danger: "terrifying," "stress," "split," "toppling," "risk," "fearfulness." Conway (in common with Hilton himself) is a skilled mountaineer and is well aware of the dangers inherent in this kind of landscape. In one sense Karakal is deeply attractive: it has a perfect shape, it is beautiful, and it completes the symmetry of the valley of Blue Moon. In another sense its beauty is illusory for it is prone to avalanches and one day may crumble, destroying the civilization below.

Literally and figuratively Karakal dominates the story. From the moment when the plane has landed Conway is drawn to it irresistibly, intrigued by its lofty remoteness and shimmering appeal. For him it symbolizes his innermost aspirations. At the same time he is aware of the fragility of his dreams. When he leaves Shangri-La at the end of the novel he looks at Karakal for the last time and reflects that

> a dream had dissolved, like all too lovely things, at the first touch of reality ... he saw the corridors of his imagination twist and strain under impact; the pavilions were toppling; all was about to be in ruins [216].

Karakal is the thematic heart of the novel, as the Palace of Green Porcelain is the heart of Wells's *The Time Machine* and the chateau is the heart of Alain-Fournier's *Le Grand Meaulnes*. The image of the mountain, remote and inaccessible, provides Hilton's narrative with a "commanding centre" — to use Henry James's terminology — which both permeates and unifies the story.

The Ending

Conway's narrative ends abruptly at the point when he, Mallinson and Lo-Tsen are about to embark on their journey from Tibet to China. The novel then concludes with an Epilogue in which Rutherford and the neurologist discuss Conway's story and try to establish whether it could be true.

The tantalizing feature of the ending is that the reader does not know what happened to Conway. We do not know whether he succeeded in finding his way back to Shangri-La, or what happened to Mallinson, or even whether Conway is still alive. We are simply left with these unanswered questions. Hilton was writing at a time when the prevailing convention was to tie up all loose ends in a novel's final chapter. In deliberately departing from this convention he leaves the reader in a state of suspense.

The significance of the Epilogue lies in the fact that both Rutherford and the neurologist are reluctant to disbelieve Conway's story and try hard to come to a conclusion about it. Rutherford summarizes the situation by saying, "It's really an exercise in the balancing of probabilities, and I must say the scales don't bump very emphatically either way. Of course, if you don't accept Conway's story, it means that you doubt either his veracity or his sanity — one may as well be frank" (228).

The novel ends with an eloquent concluding paragraph which neatly encapsulates the mood Hilton has sought to achieve throughout:

> We sat for a long time in silence, and then talked again of Conway as I remembered him, boyish and gifted and full of charm, and of the War that had altered him, and of so many mysteries of time and age and of the mind, and of the little Manchu who had been "most old," and of the strange ultimate dream of Blue Moon. "Do you think he will ever find it?" I asked [231].

This conclusion serves the same purpose as a coda in a symphony: it summarizes all that has gone before by reminding the listener of the work's main themes.

The paragraph consists of only 75 words, yet in this brief compass Hilton leaves the reader with a feeling of regretful longing which must surely be unique in twentieth century literature. Rutherford and his companion sit for a long time in silence, each remembering Conway in his own way: a mutual friend who has deeply influenced both of them. Then they talk about him, "boyish and gifted and full of charm," and discuss the 1914–1918 war which had affected Conway so much. The conversation then turns to unsolved mysteries of time and age, and turns finally to the riddle of Shangri-La and Conway's haunting story of a hidden valley lost in unexplored mountain ranges.

Hitherto the neurologist has been skeptical of Conway's story, simply commenting that it is "very remarkable," but not admitting belief. The very fact that he now asks the question "Do you think he will ever find it?" reveals that he does after all believe the story. In delaying this moment of acceptance until the last line of the novel Hilton implicitly invites us to share in this acceptance and to admit our own credulity. The last image in our minds as we close the book is that of Conway struggling to find Shangri-La and of ourselves willing him to succeed. In this way does Hilton engage our sympathies.

Dream or Reality?

Lost Horizon has been described as "an intricate interplay of illusion and reality."[7] The question we are left with at the end is: did the events described by Conway really happen? Or, to put the question another way, what is real and what is illusion?

There is an intriguing paragraph in Conway's narrative highlighting the tension between Shangri-La and the world of reality:

> He needed equanimity, if only to accommodate himself to the double life he was compelled to lead. Thenceforward, with his fellow exiles, he lived in a world conditioned by the arrival of porters and a return to India; at all other times the horizon lifted like a curtain; time expanded and space contracted, and the name Blue Moon took on a symbolic meaning.... Sometimes he wondered which of his two lives were the more real [164].

The phrase "double life" is interesting and reminds us once again that Conway is a deeply divided personality. He is divided not only in the sense that he is a man of action and a man who lives in the mind, but also in that he finds it increasingly difficult to distinguish between the "real" world and that of Shangri-La. It is arguable that a world in which "time expanded and space contracted" must be illusory and can have no basis in the world of solid fact. In saying that "sometimes he wondered which of his two lives were the more real" is not Conway recognizing the dichotomy in his own character?

During the final conversation between Conway and Mallinson (pages 200–219) Mallinson accuses him of being "completely mad" and asserts that he had "been blown up in the war, and you'd been queer at times ever since." Is there a hint here that the basis of Conway's tale — that the four passengers had been brought deliberately to the lamasery on the orders of a guiding intelligence, that the four must remain permanently at Shangri-La, and that the lamas had discovered the secret of longevity — is an illusion?

In the final analysis each reader must make his or her own choice. Hilton is in effect confronting the reader with a tantalizing riddle: which is the more "real" — Shangri-La and its entrancing mystery or the violence, ugliness and duplicity of the world outside? Conway is in no doubt which is the more real for him, for once having left Shangri-La he does his utmost to return to it.

In seeking to find his way back to the hidden lamasery is Conway merely pursuing a mirage, or is he being true to his own innermost longings?

Reading Lost Horizon

In his essay *A Gossip on Romance* R.L. Stevenson wrote:

> In anything fit to be called by the name of reading, the process itself should be absorbing and voluptuous; we should gloat over a book, be rapt clean out of ourselves, and rise from the perusal, our mind filled with the busiest, kaleidoscopic dance of images, incapable of sleep or of continuous thought.[8]

How true this is of *Lost Horizon*. The Pocket Books edition describes the book as "one of the most beloved of all modern novels." It is so highly readable and fluently told that it is easy to miss the skill with which it is written. There is also a widespread attitude in the academic world that because a novel is popular it cannot possibly be regarded as literature. In this sense it invites comparison with Daphne du Maurier's *Rebecca,* another novel which is well written and is at the same time popular with the reading public. The novelist Susan Hill said of *Rebecca*: "It can and should be read the first time with bated breath. And then read again, more calmly and carefully, for its more significant, less obvious qualities."[9] *Lost Horizon* is one of those novels which can be returned to again and again. There are many devotees who reread it annually and find new layers of meaning with each rereading. It seems assured of its place as a twentieth century classic and as a novel with a strange and continuing pull on the imagination.

9

Ideas

What kind of book is *Lost Horizon?* And on what levels can it be read?

In this chapter we will take a close look at the novel's major themes and ideas. The readings offered in this chapter are offered as possible readings only, without any sense of finality. *Lost Horizon* is so rich in hermeneutic potential that it would be presumptuous to claim that any one interpretation can be definitive. The discussion that follows offers some *pointers* to possible ways in which the story can be read.

The Reader's Expectations

In his study *Unlocking the Text: Fundamental Issues in Literary Theory,* Jeremy Hawthorn observes:

> Clearly a reader's expectations are of crucial importance to the reading process.... a literary work is never perceived innocently by a reader; to talk of seeing a literary work as it is is to ignore a range of problems arising out of variations between different reader expectations.[1]

What then are the expectations of the reader when approaching *Lost Horizon?* In the chapter on "Narrative Art" we discussed the difference between reading a novel for the first time and subsequent re-readings.

Here I want to begin by looking at the attitudes and expectations brought to the novel by an average student. It will be useful to start by considering the novel's title.

The title, as we have seen, was chosen by Hilton himself in preference to his original title, *Blue Moon.* Hilton felt that his new title was "both appropriate and attractive." The name was certainly well chosen, for the word *Lost* aptly conveys the sense of yearning experienced by Conway, a feeling of loss Hilton is clearly anxious for his readers to experience also. The word *Horizon* conveys a sense of a landscape just beyond our reach. A reader approaching the novel for the first time would be likely to assume from its title that it is a work of fantasy. Is that in fact what *Lost Horizon* is? *Chambers Twentieth Century Dictionary* defines fantasy as "a story, film, etc., not based on realistic characters or setting: preoccupation with thoughts associated with unobtainable desires." It can be seen from this definition that a reader who assumed *Lost Horizon* is a work of fantasy will have different expectations of the novel than a reader who assumes it is a realistic work. This in turn will color his opinions of the story.

My own reading of the work is that it is not a work of fantasy in the accepted sense, though it is sometimes regarded as such. I would argue that it does not describe a world of fantasy in the same sense as C.S. Lewis's Narnia or Tolkein's Middle-Earth, for the Shangri-La depicted in the novel is surely intended as a realistic description of an actual place. There is nothing magical or supernatural in Hilton's world, no mythical creatures or traveling through time. Chang and the High Lama are surely intended to be realistic portrayals of people having validity in the known world.

Because *Lost Horizon* is such a well known novel and formed the basis of a famous Hollywood film it would be difficult for a reader today to encounter the story without having heard of it before (though I have met quite literate people who claim never to have heard of James Hilton). We thus need to establish at the outset what kind of book *Lost Horizon* is. Is it a work of science fiction like (say) H.G. Wells's *The Time Machine?* Is it a satire in the vein of Swift's *Gulliver's Travels* or Voltaire's *Candide?* Or is it perhaps an allegorical fable in the same manner as Samuel Johnson's *Rasselas?*

Behind these questions lies a more fundamental point: whether the novel merits serious academic scrutiny at all. One reviewer observed, "it would be a pity to spoil one's very real pleasure in this book by taking it too seriously; it is a diversion ... none the less pleasant because it is very slight."[2] Another commentator stated: "Few reviewers expressed outright contempt for Hilton's fantasy, but none expressed the opinion that it deserved more than superficial interest."[3] Clearly if a reader regards the novel as a "diversion" possessing only superficial interest he or she is unlikely to study it with the attention it deserves. On the other hand a reader convinced that Hilton is an important writer who merits serious attention will read *Lost Horizon* with close attention to its language and meaning.

Mythology

Joseph Campbell in his study *The Hero with a Thousand Faces* has demonstrated that many of the world's myths follow a consistent pattern. First the hero arrives at the domain after an arduous journey; he crosses a threshold or barrier and enters the domain; he undergoes a series of trials or obstacles; he then leaves the domain but feels a romantic yearning for it and strives to re-enter it. Common to most myths is the notion that the hero is changed by the experience. In a chapter entitled "The Road of Trials" Campbell writes:

> Once having traversed the threshold, the hero moves in a dream landscape of curiously fluid ambiguous forms, where he must survive a succession of trials. This is a favorite phase of the myth-adventure. It has produced a world literature of miraculous tests and ordeals.[4]

It will be apparent from this description that *Lost Horizon* broadly follows the pattern of a classical myth. First, the journey itself. Time and again Hilton stresses the appalling difficulties of the journey: bitter cold, wind, sleet, snow, and treacherous mountain traverses. Conway himself is an experienced mountaineer but even he "felt at one moment that it would be impossible to go much farther." Then, the crossing of the threshold:

> Presently the ground leveled, and they stepped out of the mist into clear, sunny air. Ahead, and only a short distance away, lay the lamasery of Shangri-La [66].

The impression of having crossed a threshold is underlined by the contrast between the mist and cold of the hazardous journey and the bright sunshine of their arrival. The contrast between the almost unbearable discomforts of the journey and the peace and beauty of the lamasery is immediately striking. Despite the peace and calm of his sojourn at Shangri-La it is apparent that Conway does in fact undergo a series of trials or tests during his time there. The journey itself is a trial — not only the perilous approach to Shangri-La but the unimaginable difficulties of the return, which he seems determined to attempt. Then the death of the High Lama, surely a terrible blow after their many conversations together. Conway has come to feel deep respect for the High Lama and a sense of affinity with the mind of the aged friar. The death of the wise old man and his own succession transform his life and compel him to come to terms with his own innermost wishes. A third trial is his unrequited love for Lo-Tsen and his chagrin on finding that she loves Mallinson and not himself. His feelings toward her are deep and genuine, and in reconciling himself to her love for the younger man he turns his back on a romance which could have brought him happiness. The fourth trial is his bitter quarrel with Mallinson and his initial decision to remain at Shangri-La without him. During their quarrel hard, wounding words are spoken and each sheds his illusions about the other. It is one of the turning points in the novel and though they do succeed in patching up their differences the friendship between them can never be the same again. From this summary it is clear that *Lost Horizon* possesses many of the characteristics of a fairy tale or quest narrative: the journey, the threshold, the trial, the return. Conway is certainly changed by his experiences for it is evident that he is consumed by the desire to return to Shangri-La. For him the wish to return becomes an overriding obsession. The final drama of the death of Lo-Tsen and his own exile from the lost paradise gives to the story the dimensions of a classical tragedy. In this sense the novel can be regarded as one of the most potent twentieth century myths.

The "Lost Race"

The "lost race" fantasy forms a time honored niche in English literature. Rider Haggard's *King Solomon's Mines* (1885) and *She* (1887) are both classic examples of the genre. The early decades of the twentieth century saw the publication of a number of "lost race" narratives including Wells's "The Country of the Blind" (1904), Talbot Mundy's *Om: The Secret of the Abor Valley* (1924), D.H. Lawrence's "The Woman Who Rode Away" (1925), Ganpat's *The Mirror of Dreams* (1928) and Fowler Wright's *The Island of Captain Sparrow* (1928). Common to many "lost race" adventures is the discovery of a map or manuscript containing clues regarding the location of a lost domain, a perilous journey to an unexplored region, an encounter with an aged ruler, an escape from captivity (often accompanied by the rescue of a young woman or princess), the journey back to civilization and a regret that the lost race can never be found again. The continuing popularity of "lost race" stories suggest that narratives of this kind fill a need in the human psyche. There is undoubtedly a yearning for tales of exploration and a desire to know what the unexplored regions of the earth are like. (Note also that the sudden death of an aged mystery figure is a common feature of "lost race" narratives: witness the spectacular deaths of Gagool in *King Solomon's Mines,* Ayesha in *She* and Lo-Tsen in *Lost Horizon.*)

One reading of *Lost Horizon* then is to see it as a "lost race" narrative in a similar genre to the African romances of John Buchan and Rider Haggard. The appeal of narratives depicting lost domains and hidden kingdoms is that they satisfy the human longing for mystery and the wish to know what is on "the other side of the mountain" (a phrase actually used in the Frank Capra film version). Hilton himself uses the phrase "a lost valley in the midst of unexplored mountains" (208) which suggests that he was not immune to this yearning. Whilst freely admitting that he had not been to Tibet himself he had done extensive background reading, including descriptions of Tibet written by explorers and geographers. Much of the appeal of the novel lies in the fact that it satisfies the wish to know what Tibet is actually like.

To the end the "lost domain" remains a mystery. At the end of the novel Rutherford attempts to learn more of the mysterious mountain range where Shangri-La is supposedly located but has to admit that "I should think they must be the least explored range in the world." The idea of a "lost race" concealed behind impenetrable mountains has an undeniable appeal and answers to the romantic in the human temperament.

Contrasts

One of the main underlying themes of the novel is the contrast between Western civilization and that of the Orient. There is a continual emphasis on the contrast between two differing cultures: on the one hand, the Western world (represented by Mallinson and Barnard) with its stress on material values, ambition, haste and self-indulgence; and on the other, the Oriental world (represented by Chang and the High Lama) with its emphasis on contentment, moderation, tolerance, and lack of ambition.

The contrast is made explicit at numerous points in the narrative. When Mallinson asserts that Orientals can't be made to do anything quickly, Conway reflects that "it did not appear that the Eastern races were abnormally dilatory, but rather that Englishmen and Americans charged about the world in a state of continual and rather preposterous fever-heat" (83). On his first arrival at the lamasery Conway observes that "a separate culture might flourish here without contamination from the outside world." When Chang queries this statement Conway makes it clear that he is referring to the West's obsession with noise and garishness (71). A recurring theme in their many conversations is the contrast between the calmness, happiness and freedom from stress at Shangri-La and the dissatisfaction, haste and noise of the world outside. Chang observes: "Is there not too much tension in the world at present, and might it not be better if more people were slackers?" (168). There is a revealing episode midway through the novel when it becomes clear that Barnard is in reality a financier who is sought by the police for monkeying on Wall Street, but he himself condemns those who trusted him with their money because "they all wanted something for nothing and hadn't got the brains to get it for themselves" (123). Barnard's disillusionment with the world of high finance and the "get rich quick" mentality is another indication of Hilton's overriding theme of disenchantment with materialism. This is most strikingly apparent in the behavior of Conway himself who is increasingly attracted toward Shangri-La and all that it represents: "in a world of increasing noise and hugeness, he turned in private to gentle, precise, and miniature things" (94). When the High Lama tells Conway of his decision to entrust to him the heritage of Shangri-La, the words used by the aged ruler are significant in this context:

> My friend, it is not an arduous task that I bequeath, for our order knows only silken bonds. To be gentle and patient, to care for the riches of the mind, to preside in wisdom and secrecy while the storm rages without — it will all be very pleasantly simple for you, and you will doubtless find great happiness [197].

The key words in this passage are "gentle," "patient," "wisdom," "happiness." Notice also the phrase "to care for the riches of the mind": the contrast between this concept and the *material* riches pursued so avidly in the Western world is immediately striking. At the end of the novel when Mallinson urges Conway to leave Shangri-La and return to the outside world Conway refuses, saying quietly, "I've no desire to go back to that life at all" (209). By "that life" it is clear that he is referring to the world he and Mallinson have left behind: the world of convention and conformity in a society dominated by hedonism and the quest for power.

The key difference between the two contrasting worlds is in their respective attitudes towards *time*. When the High Lama spells out to Conway the attractions of remaining at Shangri-La he points out, "And, most precious of all, you will have Time — that rare and lovely gift that your Western countries have lost the more they have pursued it" (154). Here again the contrast between East and West is quite explicit — the difference between the notion that time is something to be savored in a calm, unhurried manner, and the idea that time is something to be pursued with feverish haste.

The clash between the differing traditions of East and West is heightened by the fact that the representatives of the two cultures are removed from their normal spheres of influence. The "Western" party — Conway, Mallinson, Barnard and Miss Brinklow — are removed from their normal surroundings and transported to a remote valley cut off from outside influences. The "Eastern" party — Chang and the High Lama — are also detached from their customary milieu as they are only seen in the context of Shangri-La and not against the conventional background of the "real" world. By removing both groups from the everyday world and placing them in a community remote from all extraneous influences Hilton sharpens the contrast between them. In this sense *Lost Horizon* can be regarded as a case study in opposing cultures: between material values, haste and intolerance on the one hand and wisdom, contentment and moderation on the other.

In common with other novels depicting a journey, *Lost Horizon* is capable of both a literal and metaphorical interpretation. Literally the novel is the story of Conway and his three companions and their journey across Tibet into the hidden community of Shangri-La. In a deeper sense it is a journey into the human mind. In finding Shangri-La, meeting the High Lama, immersing himself in a life of contemplation and then succeeding to the leadership of the community Conway finds his true vocation and in the process recognizes his inner self. Seen in these terms the novel can be read as an allegory on contrasting attitudes to life. Conway, with his love of music and reading, finds Shangri-La deeply attractive but Mallinson, with his impetuosity and indifference to culture, finds it repellent. The contrast between these two opposing attitudes colors much of the action of the novel.

The Pastoral Ideal

In one sense *Lost Horizon* can be regarded as a parable on the theme of the Garden of Eden. There is, for example, a continual emphasis on the verdant lushness of the valley. At one point the valley is described as "nothing less than an enclosed paradise of amazing fertility" in which "crops of unusual diversity grew in profusion" (106). The first sight of the valley and the lamasery reinforces the concept of a hidden paradise:

> The floor of the valley, hazily distant, welcomed the eye with greenness; sheltered from winds, and surveyed rather than dominated by the lamasery, it looked to Conway a delightfully favored place [67].

The reader is frequently reminded of the fertility of Shangri-La and its lands. Edelweiss is seen during the approach to the lamasery, mangoes and other fruits are cultivated in the valley, tuberose grows in profusion. During a conducted tour of the lamasery the party come across a beautiful garden described in terms which fix the scene in the memory:

> The party ... followed Chang through several courtyards to a scene of quite sudden and unmatched loveliness. From a colonnade steps descended to a garden, in which by some tender curiosity of irrigation a lotus-pool lay entrapped, the leaves so closely set that they gave an impression of a floor of moist green tiles [97].

The lotus is a well-known image of paradise and also symbolizes purity and enlightenment. The reiteration of romantic imagery in this passage — loveliness, garden, lotus, pool, green — underlines the notion of a pastoral idyll and prepares the reader for what follows: the first encounter with the enigmatic figure of Lo-Tsen.

The fragility of the garden paradise is emphasized at a number of points. Conway reflects that "there was a superb and exquisite peril in the scene.... The whole design was almost uncannily fortunate, so long as the structure of the frame remained unmoved by earthquake or landslide" (106). This sense of the fragility and impermanence of the lush valley strengthens the image of an enchanted idyll: a romantic concept which haunts our literature from the Arthurian legends to such tales as Alain-Fournier's *Le Grand Meaulnes.*

When the airplane crashes close to the hidden valley of Shangri-La there is a sudden and irrevocable intrusion into the green paradise. The airplane represents technology and machinery; all around is wildness and nature. In his book *The Machine in the Garden* Leo Marx states:

The sudden appearance of the machine in the garden is an arresting, endlessly evocative image. It causes the instantaneous clash of opposed states of mind.[5]

It is indeed a striking image: the abrupt arrival of the plane can be seen as an intrusion, an invasion of the enclosed paradise by "progress" and technology. The sudden juxtaposition of machinery and an undisturbed landscape is a powerful symbol and one which is characteristic of Hilton.

Culture Pocket

The idea of a separate civilization uncontaminated by Western culture has haunted English literature in the 19th and 20th centuries. From Coradine in W.H. Hudson's *A Crystal Age* (1887), Herland in Charlotte Perkins Gilman's feminist utopia of 1915 and Anares in Ursula Le Guin's *The Dispossessed* (1974) successive writers have posited the notion of an isolated community unknown to the rest of the world. Hilton takes this idea a stage further by describing a community in which literature, learning, music and art — the accumulated heritage of centuries of advancement — can be preserved: a community so remote that it will escape the destruction of a world war.

At an early stage in the novel Conway describes Shangri-La as "a separate culture isolated from the outside world" (71) and later refers to it as "this strange culture — pocket, hidden amongst unknown ranges" (101). In his conversations with Conway the High Lama repeatedly stresses the notion of the lamasery as a safe refuge isolated from contamination, a haven in which books and art treasures can be preserved against the coming holocaust. The High Lama adds: "We may expect no mercy, but we may faintly hope for neglect" (158).

Already by 1933 Hilton could sense what lay on the horizon: not only the gathering war clouds but the alarming rise of hatred and intolerance. The rise of Nazism in Germany was accompanied by book burning, destruction, mass hysteria and the manipulation of ideas on an unprecedented scale. The idea of a haven immune from war, violence and destruction was deeply attractive to Hilton. In common with his hero, Conway, Hilton was a cultured man who was widely read, loved music and was most at home in the world of the mind. Like Conway he abhorred regimentation and bigotry. Though the Nazi regime was only three months old when *Lost Horizon* was written it was already apparent that violence, intolerance and brutality were endemic. Coupled with the awesome destructive power of the airplane it was clear that civilization itself was under threat: as he would later write in *Random Harvest*, "for the first time in human history a sophisticated society faced its own extinction not theoretically in the future, but by physical death perhaps tomorrow."[6] Today, living as we do in the nuclear age, the idea of a refuge where the learning of the past can be cherished and preserved has an undeniable attraction, but in the 1930s the concept was novel and prescient. *Lost Horizon* was not by any means the first novel to predict the possible end of civilization — as long ago as 1898 Wells's *The War of the Worlds* had portrayed a haunting vision of the crumbling of organized society — but it was one of the first to put forward the idea of a "safe haven" where mankind's cultural heritage could be conserved.

Utopia

Lost Horizon follows on in a long established literary tradition: that of the utopian novel. The word "Utopia" (Greek for "no place") was coined by Sir Thomas More in his work of that name published in 1516, but the tradition is of course much older. From Plato's *Republic* onward (circa 387 B.C.) writers have sought to criticize existing society by projecting imaginary worlds. What is the purpose of utopian literature?

In a perceptive essay the academic William Kenney has observed:

> The utopia depicted in fiction can serve as a model by which the real world and real societies can be judged. By presenting his vision of utopia, the writer urges the real world to cleanse itself of its imperfections, to lessen the gap between what is and what should be.[7]

It may be objected that, unlike previous utopias such as Plato's *Republic* and twentieth century examples such as B.F. Skinner's *Walden Two*

(1948) and Aldous Huxley's *Island* (1962), the society described in *Lost Horizon* is insufficiently detailed to be regarded as a fully worked out model of an ideal community. In this sense *Lost Horizon* is not a detailed utopia such as Bellamy's *Looking Backward* (1888), where every facet of government and commerce is described. What Hilton does succeed in doing remarkably well is to give an *impression* of a community that is happy, harmonious and productive. He does this by creating an atmosphere of contentment: an atmosphere in which any hint of violence or discord would seem utterly incongruous.

The population of the valley, for example, are described as "good humoured and mildly inquisitive, courteous and care-free, busy at innumerable jobs but not in any apparent hurry over them. Altogether Conway thought them one of the pleasantest communities he had ever seen" (107). Later he speculates as to the manner in which the valley people are governed:

> He was particularly interested, as a student of affairs, in the way
> the valley population was governed; it appeared, on examination to
> be a rather loose and elastic autocracy, operated from the lamasery
> with a benevolence that was almost casual [113].

The word "autocracy" may jar with a 21st century reader, but there are two points to notice about this statement. The first is that the government is "loose and elastic": the valley is ruled with benevolence and only moderate strictness. The second and more important point is that in describing an ideal community governed by an enlightened minority Hilton was following a long established literary and utopian tradition. The Guardians of Plato's *Republic,* the paternalistic government of More's *Utopia,* the priest-philosophers of Campanella's *City of the Sun* (1623) and the paternalistic rulers of Francis Bacon's *The New Atlantis* (1627) are all examples of enlightened minorities exercising power. It should also be noted that the society depicted in *Lost Horizon* is the antithesis of the regimented communities described in *Looking Backward* and *Walden Two.* The inhabitants of Shangri-La — both those in the lamasery and in the valley below — are happy, contented and free from stress, a fact which Hilton underlines:

> Certainly during visits to the valley Conway found a spirit of
> goodwill and contentment that pleased him all the more because he
> knew that of all the arts that of government has been brought least
> to perfection [114].

We are told that the population of the lamasery is about fifty, and that the population of the valley is several thousand. Would such an ideal society only work in a small community? Could such an ideal community exist at all? Shangri-La, we are told, has no crime, no police, no armed forces and no prisons. Is the novel "utopian" in the sense that it is impracticable? One of the reasons why *Lost Horizon* has always been so popular is that the community portrayed within it is so attractive. It is because of this that "Shangri-La" has become part of the English language and has come to mean any ideal place, a refuge from the stresses of the world. Opinions will differ as to the feasibility or otherwise of the society described in its pages, but this does not detract from Hilton's achievement in creating this utopia and describing it with such total conviction. In his study of myths of sacred landscapes Peter Bishop observed that:

> Hilton's novel *Lost Horizon* ... was the quintessence of a Tibetan
> utopia. It had an essential authenticity about it — not in the sense
> of being empirically feasible, but of conforming to the reality of
> contemporary fantasies about Tibet.[8]

Many readers will have their own personal vision of a "great good place," an idyll where harmony reigns and which is remote from all contamination. In translating this dream into tangible form Hilton gives fictional expression to one of our deepest desires.

Seen in these terms it can be seen that *Lost Horizon* is a classical example of the genre for it explicitly contrasts the world outside Shangri-La with the society contained within it. The four newcomers to Shangri-La have fled from Baskul where they encountered revolution, war, and torture. When Mallinson claims that the situation in Baskul was "healthier" than at Shangri-La, Conway reminds him that they were up against murder and rape. At the end of the novel when Rutherford is seeking to establish the truth of Conway's story he visits Shanghai and describes the terrible air-raids during the war with Japan. The ideal society depicted in the novel is thus contrasted with the violence, disorder and intolerance of the world outside it. When an interviewer asked Hilton how *Lost Horizon* came to be written, he replied: "At the back of my mind I have a feeling that it is the duty of every writer to deal with the current problems and the anomalies he finds around him."[9] In depicting a utopian society seen by apparently real characters in an apparently real location Hilton implicitly criticizes society as he saw it in the 1930s and offers an alternative vision of how life might be.

His own attitude toward his utopia is not in doubt. He clearly finds it deeply attractive and wishes his readers to share his enthusiasm for it and Conway's desolating sense of loss. Whether the reader finds it attractive will depend on his perception of the novel. Is Hilton describing a place which has, or *could* have, a basis in reality? Or is it simply a dream, a piece of escapism?

It is worth drawing attention to the fact that, despite Conway's unmistakable yearning for Shangri-La and all that it represents, at the end of the story he deliberately turns his back on it and walks away. His bitter regret at doing so does not alter the fundamental truth that he is prepared to leave it. Does Hilton implicitly reject his own utopia? One of the tantalizing questions left in the mind after reading the novel is that of Conway's ultimate attitude toward the world he is describing. As he himself expresses it: "He did not know whether he had been mad and was now sane, or had been sane for a time and was now mad again" (216).

This raises the question, who is the greater realist, Conway or Mallinson? It could be argued that in wishing to return to Shangri-La Conway is neglecting his responsibilities in the real world and pursuing an empty dream. Those who take this view would argue that it is Mallinson who is the greater realist for he is prepared to accept the world for what it is— imperfect, but still worth living in. Those who take the opposite view would assert that Mallinson is indifferent to the things of the mind. Utopian novels can be stimulating precisely because they generate questions of this kind.

The novel is not only about a utopia in the sense that it depicts an ideal community but also in that it describes a valley which is rich in gold. It thus resembles the fabled El Dorado, a sought-after land of wealth and treasure. Shangri-La is a unique place, a *locus* which only a privileged few can ever find. When Conway sees it for the first time it seems to him that he has reached at last "some place that was an end, a finality" (67). Chang explains later that to leave the valley means certain death, and adds: "There is only one valley of Blue Moon, and those who expect another are asking too much of nature" (166). There is a powerful sense of a lost idyll, a Holy Grail which shimmers elusively on the horizon.

The creation and elaboration of utopias forms an honourable part of world literatures. H.G. Wells, who himself wrote numerous utopian novels including *A Modern Utopia* (1905) and *Men Like Gods* (1923), asserted: "I think, in fact, that the creation of utopias — and their exhaustive criticism — is the proper and distinctive method of sociology."[10] One of the most valuable functions served by utopian novels is to project an alternative canvas of society and in doing so to offer a critique of the normal, "real" world.

It should be noted that in holding out the prospect of an ideal society *Lost Horizon* was in some ways running counter to the mood of the time. Zamyatin in *We* (1920) and Aldous Huxley in *Brave New World* (1932) had both posited a regimented, soulless society and depicted a basically pessimistic view of human nature. Both novels held out little, if any, prospect of hope for the future. Kafka in *The Trial* (1925) and Hesse in *Steppenwolf* (1927) had dwelt on the emptiness of modern civilization and the suppression of individuality. Hilton's novel, in contrast, can be regarded as an affirmation of the human spirit. It implicitly rejects the dystopian vision of these works and emphasizes such values as tolerance and compassion in place of pessimism and despair. Behind *Lost Horizon* is a value judgement of fundamental importance — that human life, for all its trials and shortcomings, is worth living; and that human betterment is a goal worth striving for. This judgment is inherent in all Hilton's work and reaches its apotheosis in *Lost Horizon*.

The End of Certainty

In his "Chapter of Autobiography" written in 1938 Hilton observed apropos of his schooling:

> To make up for all I have forgotten, there is this that I have
> acquired, and I call it sophistication since it is not quite the same
> thing as learning. It is the flexible armour of doubt in an age when
> too many people are certain.[11]

This stress on "the flexible armour of doubt" is characteristic of Hilton and might almost be described as the underlying philosophy of *Lost Horizon*. When Conway asks Chang to explain the motivation behind Shangri-La, Chang replies:

> If I were to put it into a very few words, my dear sir, I should say
> that our prevalent belief is in moderation. We inculcate the virtue
> of avoiding excess of all kinds — even including, if you will pardon
> the paradox, excess of virtue itself [74].

Later, when Conway observes that there does not seem to be any democratic machinery at Shangri-La. Chang replies: "Oh no, our people would be quite shocked by having to declare that one policy was completely right and another completely wrong" (115).

It is difficult for us today — living, as we do, in an age of doubt and ambiguity — to recapture the passionate certainties of political debate in the 1930s. The decade was one of fierce argument on the pros and cons of democracy, socialism, communism, fascism, anarchism and pacifism. In such an atmosphere it was difficult if not impossible to be neutral. Whatever one's political stance, one was inevitably caught up in these ideological debates; one took sides. In complete contrast the entire philosophy of *Lost Horizon* is one of toleration and moderation. This attitude of respect for others beliefs and an unwillingness to adopt dogmatic stances — an attitude wholly opposed by Miss Brinklow, who is convinced that she alone possesses a monopoly of the truth — has to be seen against the background of the atmosphere of the time. It was an age of *certainty*. One was either *for* something or *against* it. The philosophy of toleration exemplified by Shangri-La and its inhabitants flew in the face of prevailing attitudes.

10

Film Versions
and Other Adaptations

For more than 70 years *Lost Horizon* has been available as a much loved novel and is familiar to many readers in this form. In common with other classic novels the story has been adapted into other media including film, radio and stage. This chapter takes a closer look at these versions and discusses the extent to which they can be regarded as reliable adaptations. In the process we will look at some of the problems involved in translating a best selling novel into alternative formats.

The 1937 Film Version

Cast List

Robert Conway	Ronald Colman
George Conway	John Howard
Henry Barnard	Thomas Mitchell
Gloria Stone	Isabel Jewell
Alexander P. Lovett	Edward Everett Horton
Chang	H.B. Warner
High Lama	Sam Jaffe
Sondra Bizet	Jane Wyatt
Maria	Margo
Director	Frank Capra
Executive Producer	Harry Cohn

Screenplay	Robert Riskin
Musical Score	Dimitri Tiomkin

There can be no question that the Frank Capra film version richly deserves its reputation as one of the outstanding motion pictures of the twentieth century and amply merits the superlatives heaped upon it. Lawrence J. Quirk in *The Great Romantic Films* states: "There is no denying that this first film transcription of the James Hilton novel is a whale of a movie—inspirational, exciting, well acted, unusual, a film with a 'message' all audiences found not only palatable but fantastically entertaining as well." R. Dixon Smith in *Ronald Colman, Gentleman of the Cinema* described the film as "a soaring, fantastic poem of flight from chaos to tranquility," while Juliet Benita Colman in her biography of her father hails it as "a heart-lifting, ageless story—and cast, script, production and direction do Hilton's novel proud."[1]

All conspires to achieve a film of genuine stature. Frank Capra's assured direction, a highly literate script by Robert Riskin, a splendid musical score by Dimitri Tiomkin, the memorable acting of Ronald Colman, and above all a haunting story by James Hilton fuse together to produce an impressive film which lingers long in the mind. Today most viewers will watch the film on video or DVD, sitting at home and seeing it on a television screen. Seen in this way it remains an impressive movie, but it must have been doubly spectacular to watch it on a big screen in a cinema, surrounded by all the panoply of the golden age of Hollywood: the art deco architecture, the excitement of the audience, the parting of the curtains, the dimming of the lights as the "big picture" commenced. The film critic John Baxter commented: "*Lost Horizon* is one of the most impressive of all thirties films, a splendid fantasy which, physically and emotionally, lets out all the stops."[2] *Lost Horizon* received no fewer than seven Academy Award nominations including Best Picture, Best Film Editing and Best Interior Decoration.

Frank Capra was a young American director who had been active in Hollywood since 1921. He had directed a number of highly successful silent comedies and with the advent of "talkie" films had directed some outstanding productions including *Dirigible* (1931), *The Bitter Tea of General*

Yen (1932) and *Broadway Bill* (1933). He then turned his attention to social comedies with an underlying seriousness of purpose; these include *It Happened One Night* (1934) and *Mr. Deeds Goes to Town* (1936), for both of which he won Academy Awards. Capra was widely respected as an original and enterprising director who could be relied upon to produce films of innovation and quality. Robert Riskin had also had a distinguished career and was responsible for some of Hollywood's most sparkling scripts including *The Miracle Woman* (1931) and *Lady for a Day* (1933). Dimitri Tiomkin, then in his late thirties, was a young and relatively untried composer who was later to achieve fame for his scores of *High Noon* (1952) and *The Guns of Navarone* (1961). For *Lost Horizon* he produced a haunting and evocative score which from the first moments of the film conveys a mood of mystical power. Capra, Riskin and Tiomkin worked together as a team, often involving Ronald Colman in their discussions to ensure that all those principally involved shared a common concept of the film.

The film's maker, Columbia, went to great pains to ensure that the film should be as technically accurate as possible. The American explorer and photographer Harrison Forman was appointed technical director in charge of research work. In this capacity he made an extensive study of Tibetan life and culture including research into lamaseries, costumes, architecture, language, furniture and musical instruments, visiting Tibet for this purpose and bringing back a huge archive of photographs and documents. Every detail of Tibetan life was replicated in the studio including clothing, hairstyles, decorations and implements. This research took one year, while simultaneously Frank Capra and Robert Riskin worked on the script and grappled with the problem of how to bring the novel to the screen.

The spectacular Shangri-La sets were constructed in Hollywood and conceived by the art director Stephen Goosson; the series of sets was one of the costliest and largest ever constructed and even rivaled those made for the Biblical epics of D.W. Griffith. For the plane journey across the Tibetan mountains genuine footage of the Himalayas was used as a backdrop, while the snow scenes were filmed inside an ice-house to ensure that the snow and ice should not only *look* realistic but be the real thing. Altogether Capra spent $2,500,000 on the project: an immense sum of money

139

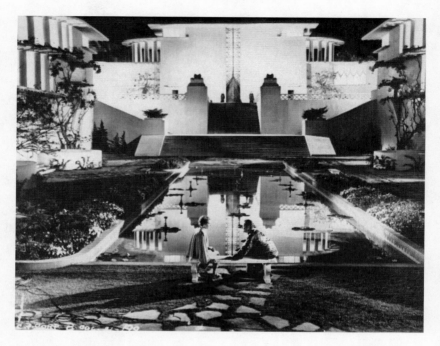

Ronald Colman (Conway) and Jane Wyatt (Sondra) are seated by a lotus pool at Shangri-La in the Frank Capra film version of *Lost Horizon* (courtesy R. Dixon Smith).

for 1937, especially bearing in mind that Columbia was one of the least wealthy Hollywood studios.

When it came to casting Capra was in no doubt that he wanted Ronald Colman to play the part of Conway. Capra wrote:

> I could see only one person in the role of Conway and that was Colman. Ronald was English, a perfect gentleman and above all, he was an idealist with a tough mind — the perfect combination that would justify the High Lama's kidnapping him from the world and bringing him to Shangri-La as his successor.[3]

In any event this proved to be a wise decision, for Colman's performance in the key role of Conway is sincere, polished and memorable. It is Colman's performance which *makes* the film by its integrity and strength.

Ronald Colman (Conway) and Jane Wyatt (Sondra) are deep in conversation in the Frank Capra film version of *Lost Horizon* (courtesy R. Dixon Smith).

Some of the acting by John Howard (as his brother George) and Isabel Jewell (as Gloria) seems melodramatic and amateurish in comparison, but Colman plays to perfection the role of the English gentleman who becomes enchanted by Shangri-La and is agonized by having to face the decision of whether to leave. Consider, for example, the scene toward the end of the film where George is trying to persuade him to abandon Shangri-La. Without any histrionics Colman vividly conveys the dilemma of a man who is tormented by doubts: emotionally he longs to remain at Shangri-La, yet intellectually he senses that his brother is right and that his duty lies in returning to the outside world. Another example is the scene a little later when he looks back at the valley of Blue Moon and surveys Shangri-La for the last time. Into his eyes and facial expression Colman conveys all the longing of a man who is parting irrevocably from all that means most to him and is filled with inappeasable regrets. These are simply two instances which have been chosen as an illustration of Colman's abilities as an actor. The entire film is dominated by his presence. He told Capra that he felt he was not simply *acting* the part of Conway but that he actually *was* Conway: he felt he was really inside the part, sharing Conway's dreams, thoughts and emotions.

For the High Lama Capra chose a little known actor named Sam Jaffe, who was in fact only 38 but movingly takes the part of a man of advanced age. Jaffe had little film experience but had been on stage since 1916. With his whispering voice and expressive eyes he vividly conveys the image of the aged lama who is anxious to meet Conway and entrust to him the heritage and destiny of Shangri-La. For the important role of Chang Capra chose the British actor H.B. Warner, who plays the part of the "prime minister" of Shangri-La with immense dignity and presence. Capra felt it was important that the actors taking the part of the lamasery inhabitants should be little known, thus heightening the atmosphere of strangeness, and for that reason chose Sam Jaffe, H.B. Warner and Jane Wyatt, none of whom was widely known. This contrasts with the passengers on the plane — played by Ronald Colman, Thomas Mitchell and Edward Everett Horton — all of whom would have been familiar faces to cinema audiences. For Jane Wyatt, who took the part of Sondra Bizet — the attractive young girl with whom Conway falls in love — this was only her second film role and she was just 24. She brought to the role of Sondra an engaging freshness and appeal.

What was Hilton's own involvement in the film? It is known that he discussed the screenplay with Capra and Riskin and also visited the set on a number of occasions, talking to members of the cast. In an article he wrote about his Hollywood experiences he stated:

> I first met Capra at Frances Marion's house a few days after I arrived in Hollywood. We then talked for two hours about *Lost Horizon:* he explained and described his ideas about making a screenplay of it and the changes (most of them slight) that seemed advisable to him and to Robert Riskin, who was writing the script. I found him in complete sympathy with the mood and spirit of the story.[4]

The film critic Leslie Halliwell in his book *Halliwell's Hundred: A Nostalgic Choice of Films from the Golden Age* comments that many writers would have been outraged at the changes made to the story but adds that "most were said to have won the approval of James Hilton, who allegedly wished he had thought of them first."[5]

All the indications are that Hilton liked and admired the Capra film and considered it to be a splendid realization of his story. From his point of view it brought the story to the attention of a huge audience, many of whom may not have read the original novel.

The film is rich in memorable images: the airplane flight across the frozen mountain ranges, the hazardous journey to Shangri-La when the four passengers are roped together, the first sight of the hidden valley and the soaring lamasery buildings, the death of the High Lama, the parting from Shangri-La and the sudden aging of Maria (an echo of the sudden aging of Lo-Tsen implied in the novel), and finally the unforgettable closing scene when Conway sees Shangri-La once again. These images, accompanied by Dimitri Tiomkin's haunting music, the spectacular backdrop of the lamasery and some fine acting combine to achieve a film which lingers long in the mind.

The abrupt transformation of Maria from vibrant youth to a woman of advanced age is a truly terrifying moment. Against a background of howling winds, and frozen wastes Conway, George and Maria are struggling to keep up with the porters and seek temporary shelter in a cave. Maria is utterly exhausted and pleads that she can go no further. George stares at her in horrified disbelief and then calls out "Bob! Bob! Her face! Look at her face!" The camera then focuses on the wrinkled face and white hair of an old woman. Appalled by what he has seen George is overcome with hysteria and plunges to his death down a precipice. This is one of the most dramatic moments in the film, made all the more poignant by the fact that Maria is played by the young Spanish actress Margo, who was then 19. Her sudden aging confirms the truth of all that Conway has been told about Shangri-La and proves conclusively that in claiming to be young Maria has lied to George. This moment of revelation remains in the mind long after the film has come to an end. I myself first saw the film when I was very young but this scene is one of the moments I cannot forget.

One of the great strengths of the Capra film is the striking contrast it portrays between Shangri-La itself and the world outside. The opening sequence in the war-torn city of Baskul presents a scene of conflict, violence, confusion and noise. This is followed by the plane journey across a desolate snowscape of rugged mountains and windswept plains. When the plane crashes the stranded passengers find themselves marooned in an inhospitable terrain of howling winds, snow flurries, emptiness and desolation. Then comes the journey to the lamasery, a perilous trek across a mountain traverse assailed by wind, sleet, mist and bitter cold. The sharp contrast between this world and the world of Shangri-La could not be more marked. On their arrival Conway gazes in wonderment at the peace and seclusion of the hidden valley, and stares in awe at the spectacular architecture of the lamasery buildings. Instead of cold, desolation, hunger and unknown dangers the party are surrounded by peace, harmony and comfort. On every hand they see evidence of a benign intelligence and the balm of kindness and order. When, at the end of the film, Conway and his two companions leave Shangri-La, we see the same process in reverse. The peace and orderliness of life at the lamasery is immediately contrasted with the bitter cold and savage wind of the icy wastes outside the valley. Audiences watching the film in 1937, when depression and unemployment were widespread, responded eagerly to its message of hope. The film's final words, "Here's my hope that Robert Conway will find his Shangri-La; here's my hope that we *all* find our Shangri-La," must have struck an echo with thousands of viewers. In contrasting so vividly the "real" world of war, violence, anger and unhappiness with the "ideal" world depicted in *Lost Horizon* the movie threw into sharp relief the possibility of a better and happier world. In doing so it offered its audience a message of hope and provided an aspiration which ensured the film's popularity for decades.

There can be no doubt that the film has done much to popularize the concept of Shangri-La. Thousands of viewers (possibly millions if one includes the television screenings and the video and DVD copies) base their knowledge of Shangri-La on the movie, without having read the novel. Many viewers are probably unaware that the story was written by James Hilton. To many it is simply a classic story, popularized in movies and house names. To these viewers "Shangri-La" is simply another name for "Utopia": an idyll remote from the everyday world. Whatever reservations one may have about the Capra film version this much can be claimed on its behalf: it has done more to popularize the idea of Shangri-La than any other film or book and seems destined to have a permanent place in the history of motion pictures.

It is important to bear in mind that there is a fundamental difference between reading a novel and watching a film, and this is especially true of a story containing elements of fantasy. When reading *Lost Horizon* Shangri-La exists only in the reader's imagination: each reader will have his or her own mental concept of what Shangri-La looks like. When watching a film version *nothing* is left to the imagination: the lamasery depicted on the screen is *the film studio's idea* of how it should look. This may or may not correspond with our own mental picture. The 1937 film has now acquired such classic status that the lamasery sets are regarded as the definitive version of Shangri-La. We need to remind ourselves that this is simply one possible version and that both reader and viewer are free to imagine alternative concepts if they so wish. Hilton himself was pleased with Capra's vision, for he wrote later, "Capra's conception of the lamasery at Shangri-La, that tranquil Tibetan refuge from the troubles of the world, was more visual than mine had ever been; but henceforth it is part of my own mental conception also."[6]

In what way is the 1937 film version an improvement on the novel? There are in my view two main respects in which the Capra film can be regarded as enhancing the conviction of Hilton's novel. The first of these is the decision to replace the "Mallinson" character with Conway's younger brother. This makes much more feasible Conway's decision to accompany him in leaving Shangri-La. In the novel Conway and Mallinson are not related at all: the link between them is simply that of consul and vice consul. Although we are told that the two are friends and that the older man is fond of Mallinson it still seems unlikely that Conway would have deliberately turned his back on Shangri-La and all that it represents simply in order to help his young colleague cross a difficult mountain traverse. However fond Conway is of Mallinson it stretches credulity too far to suppose that he would have abandoned all his dreams and longings to help his impetuous colleague. It simply does not ring true. The situation depicted in the film seems much more plausible: that in deciding to leave Shangri-La he is helping his own brother to escape from a situation he finds intolerable.

The other main respect in which the film improves on the novel is the idea that Conway has been *deliberately* chosen and brought to Shangri-La, not by chance as in the novel. In the film it is Sondra who recommends to the High Lama that Conway should be brought to the lamasery, for both she and the High Lama have read Conway's books and admired their underlying philosophy, especially his statement that "There are moments in every man's life when he glimpses the eternal." It does seem much more plausible that Conway has been specifically chosen to be brought to the lamasery because of his outstanding qualities and because he can contribute to the lamasery's work. It is arguably a weakness of the novel that in the original story it is purely a matter of chance that he is a passenger on the plane, especially bearing in mind that Conway is such an unusual, charismatic man and that he is eventually chosen as the High Lana's successor.

In what way is the Capra film version inferior to the novel? Or, to put the question another way, which aspects of the novel are lost in translating it to the screen? Novel and film are two very different mediums and it is perhaps inevitable that much of the novel's philosophical element is lost or oversimplified in the screen version, though to be fair to Riskin's script it has to be said that some of the dialogue — especially in the conversations between Conway and the High Lama — is taken almost word for word from the novel. There are a number of incongruities in the film — for example, the statement that the High Lama, Father Perrault, amputated his own leg when he first stumbled into the valley of Blue Moon. This surely invites disbelief. It is also difficult to believe Maria's claim that she has been stealing gold and that these thefts have been undetected.

The main weakness of the film in my own view is the addition of the "fussy paleontologist" character Alexander P. Lovett, played by Edward Everett Horton. Opinions on this character differ sharply. In his filmography of Ronald Colman R. Dixon Smith states: "The addition of the Lovett character ... was inspired, and resulted in some of the wittiest dialogue sequences Robert Riskin ever wrote."[7] I can only say that I personally find this character childish and irritating, and cannot help feeling that the film would be better without him. Horton introduces a risible element into the film which detracts from its serious message, and from this standpoint is an irrelevance. It was also a mistake to dispense with the Miss Brinklow character — who for all her waspishness and narrow mindedness is an important character in her own right — and to replace her with a prostitute suffering from tuberculosis, a role played in an "over the top" manner by Isabel Jewell.

As originally conceived the Capra film had a running time of 150 minutes, thirty minutes longer than the standard duration of a full-length feature film. The film began with a prologue showing Conway returning to Britain on board ship and meeting the famous pianist Sieveking. Conway plays some Chopin pieces which he insists were taught to him by a former pupil of Chopin's. When his listeners express incredulity Conway's memories of Shangri-La return to him and he sets out on his journey to try and find it again. When Capra realized that a 150 minute film was too long he simply eliminated the prologue and released the film with a running time of 132 minutes, then cut it again for its general release to a length of 118 minutes. Among the scenes deleted were part of the conversation between Conway and his brother on the plane, some badinage between Barnard and Lovett, and some scenes between Conway and Sondra. In 1942 Columbia released the film again (this time under the title *Lost Horizon of Shangri-La*) with a reduced time of 107 minutes, and in 1952 with a further reduction to 90 minutes. The film historian Robert Gitt of the American Film Institute spent 13 years of detective work in tracking down the lost footage and in 1986 the AFI released a restored version reconstructing the missing scenes with the use of stills to fill any remaining gaps. The significance of this version is that it restores the entire 132 minute soundtrack as originally intended. It is this version which is widely known in video and DVD format, as a "Columbia Classic." One can only agree with Columbia's description of the movie as "this lavishly produced classic about the enchanted paradise of Shangri-La where time stands still." *Lost Horizon* remains in the mind as one of those classic films which epitomize the golden age of Hollywood. It has everything: adventure, excitement, suspense, mystery, romance, sadness and happiness. It is one of those films which merits repeated viewings as a story for all time.

The 1973 Film Version

Cast List

Richard Conway	Peter Finch
George Conway	Michael York
Catherine	Liv Ullman
Chang	John Gielgud
High Lama	Charles Boyer
Maria	Olivia Hussey
Lovett	Bobbie Vann
Director	Charles Jarratt
Screenplay	Larry Kramer
Musical Score	Burt Bacharach

The 1973 movie version faithfully follows the storyline of the Capra film and replicates almost intact much of its dialogue. All the "set pieces" of the earlier version are replicated here: the violent beginning at Baskul airport, the plane journey to Tibet, the trek to Shangri-La, the conversations with the High Lama, the escape from Shangri-La, the sudden aging of Maria, the hysteria and death of Conway's brother — all these are present, with the added dimension of color instead of black and white. What mars this version in my view is the interpolation of a series of songs of utter banality. If the songs are edited out (for example by "fast forwarding" on a video player), what remains is a more than passable version of Hilton's story.

Peter Finch gives a sincere performance as Conway, though he cannot match the integrity and conviction of Colman's interpretation. Charles Boyer is a memorable High Lama and admirably conveys the sense of presence required by this role. One shares Finch's feeling of reverence in meeting this benign and wise ruler. John Gielgud is perfectly cast as Chang and brings authority and dignity to this important role. It is unfortunate that the excellence of these performances is not matched by the remainder of the cast, much of whose acting seems wooden and uninspired by comparison.

The musical version has been almost universally panned by critics. Leonard Maltin in his authoritative *Movie and Video Guide* comments: "The first half hour copies the 1937 film scene for scene, and everything's fine; then we get to Shangri-La and awful Burt Bacharach–Hal David songs, and it falls apart." The *Radio Times Guide to Films* states: "In his 1937 adaptation Frank Capra managed to make sense of the fanciful ideas raised in James Hilton's novel, but they are rendered risible in this ill-conceived musical remake." Leslie Halliwell in his *Film Guide* comments acidly: "Torpid remake with a good opening followed by slabs of philosophizing dialogue and an unbroken series of tedious songs." Lawrence Quirk in *The Great Romantic Films* simply states: "A musical version of *Lost Horizon* was produced in 1973, and the less said about it the better.... An uneasy blend of not very tuneful songs and dull romanticizing."[8]

Despite these adverse comments the musical version is worth watching for several reasons. The vivid color is in sharp contrast to the monochrome of the 1937 version and heightens the drama and spectacle of the story: this is particularly true of the scenes in Baskul and during the epic journey across the mountain ranges. It is also worth seeing for the acting of Charles Boyer, John Gielgud and Peter Finch, each of whom in his own way brings realism and conviction to their roles. The earlier version has become so familiar and has acquired such classic status that it is easy to accept its interpretation of the story as definitive. From this aspect alone it is useful to have a different version for purposes of comparison. Though marred in my judgment by its trite songs the 1973 remake has moments of genuine power. Even for those who find the music irritating the film remains interesting and watchable for the simple reason that it tells an exciting story which no amount of banality can diminish.

Novel to Film

As we have seen in the "Narrative Art" and "Ideas" sections, *Lost Horizon* is a novel which can be read on several different levels. In one sense it is an exciting tale of adventure, describing an epic journey across unexplored mountains and the discovery of a lost valley hidden in the remotest part of Tibet. In another sense it is a novel with a *thoughtful* dimension: it contains lengthy conversations on philosophy and ideas, and whole passages describing Conway's beliefs and thought processes. How much of this can be translated to the screen?

Hilton discussed this point with Capra and wrote later: "I was inclined for more changes than he was, for I wanted to shorten rather drastically some of the High Lama's speeches, whereas Capra believed he could keep more of them intact."[9] It is clear that Capra and Riskin tried hard to retain a philosophical dimension (this is particularly evident in the restored version now available on DVD) but in transforming a complex novel into a two-hour entertainment much of Hilton's language and literary skill has been lost. Take for instance the following passage from Chapter 5:

> Conway alone submitted to a rich and growing enchantment. It was not so much any individual thing that attracted him as the gradual revelation of elegance, of modest and impeccable taste, of harmony so fragrant that it seemed to gratify the eye without arresting it [93].

How is it possible to render this in cinematic terms? It cannot be done. All that can be done is to *suggest* Conway's enchantment with Shangri-La (which the Capra film undoubtedly does) but a screen version, however competently done, cannot replicate the experience of reading the novel. One of the reasons that reading *Lost Horizon* is such enjoyable experience is that it is so well written: Hilton's language is a pleasure to read. His style is smooth and flowing, and his language is carefully chosen to achieve an atmosphere of ethereal beauty. No film version can be a substitute for that of reading the story on the printed page. A film can add a new dimension but it cannot replace the intellectual and emotional satisfaction of studying the novel.

Radio Adaptations

In the late 1940s Hilton was invited to select the material to be dramatized for the "Playhouse" series of plays on American radio. For some years he selected and presented the plays, often acting as narrator. He became so interested in the workings of radio that he sat in on all the program conferences. Radio adaptations of his own *Lost Horizon* and *Goodbye Mr. Chips* were featured in the series. *Lost Horizon* has been frequently adapted as a radio play in both Britain and the United States. The story lends itself surprisingly well to the broadcast medium. If one recalls the dramatic highlights in the story — the journey by plane, the encounter with Chang, the arrival at Shangri-La, the conversations with the High Lama, the arguments between Conway and Mallinson and the decision to leave Shangri-La — it will readily be seen that these can be highly effective in audio form for radio. With appropriate sound effects such as howling winds and Tibetan musical instruments a play based on the story can work with remarkable conviction.

Of all the radio versions of *Lost Horizon* perhaps the best is the one featuring Ronald Colman as Conway. This was broadcast by the Columbia Broadcasting System in the U.S. on 15 September 1941 in the Lux Radio Theater, Hollywood, and ran for 46 minutes. It was introduced by Cecil B. De Mille. The cast was as follows:

Hugh Conway	Ronald Colman
Charles Mallinson	Dennis Green
High Lama	Donald Crisp
Lo Tsen	Lynne Carver
Chang	Cy Kendall
Rutherford	Dennis Hoey
Barnard	Dick Elliot
Miss Brinklow	Jill Esmond
Talu	Charlie Lung
Sieveking	Peter Leeds

This adaptation is remarkably faithful to the novel and captures the essence of the book with dramatic impact. Ronald Colman is totally convincing in the central part and powerfully conveys Conway's yearning for Shangri-La, while Donald Crisp as the High Lama gives an unforgettable portrayal of a man of wisdom looking back on his long life. In 1984 the play was made available as a recording (Radiola Record 51R-1148, drama series no. 7; release no. 148). This version can be strongly recommended as an accurate adaptation of the story. With a running time of only three quarters of an hour it is inevitable that the story is simplified, yet it distills the novel into a powerful and haunting entertainment which remains so even after repeated hearings.

The Stage Musical

In 1954 James Hilton collaborated with Jerome Lawrence, Robert E Lee and Harry Warren on a stage musical called *Shangri-La,* based on the novel. Hilton helped with the adaptation of the book and co-wrote the lyrics of some of the many songs which featured in the show. The show premiered in April 1956. The provincial tour was quite successful, but it only ran on Broadway for three weeks, partly as a result of the New York subway strike, which also adversely affected other productions that summer. The musical starred Lew Ayres, Martyn Green and Harold Lang.

In October 1954 Lawrence and Lee had traveled to England to discuss the possibility of staging their show in the West End, and had talks with Noel Coward, Michael Redgrave and Sir Cedric Hardwicke, but nothing came of this. Hilton's death in December 1954 no doubt cast a shadow over the project.

Once the show had been written Warren, Lawrence and Lee devised a concert version which was performed by five singers, pianist and reader for potential financial backers as they tried to raise the capital for staging their production. With hindsight, Warren felt that perhaps this intimate small-scale format was more suited to the material than a fully-staged production. The musical's first performance was on 21 April 1956 at the Shubert Theater, New Haven. It was performed by a cast which included some relatively well-known performers — Lew Ayres, character actress Alice Ghostley — as well as some promising young artists — dancer Harold Lang, singer Carol Lawrence — with costumes designed by Irene Sharaff, choreography by Donald Saddler and orchestrations by Philip J Lang. The program for this opening performance shows that 19 songs were featured, as well as several dance sequences. *Variety* (25 October 1960) stated that the production "showed spirit, imagination and had a philosophical quality without being the least bit sermonizing," although the music was felt to be too delicate and ethereal. In 1960 the musical was adapted for television by Lawrence and Lee, as part of NBC's "Hallmark Hall of Fame" series.[10] The musical version never really "caught on," possibly because it was out of step with the mood of the time. Popular musicals in the 1950s were *The Most Happy Fella* (1956) and *My Fair Lady* (1957), while the films of the moment included *The King and I, Love Me Tender* and *Rock around the Clock*. The gentle, whimsical mood of the musical was perhaps too other worldly for the hard-bitten 1950s.

Audiocassettes

In 1995 the British firm Soundings Audio Services issued the full text of *Lost Horizon* on 5 audiocassettes with a total running time of seven and a half hours. The text is read with fluency and authority by Christopher Kay. This series of tapes can be strongly recommended to those who prefer to *listen* to the text of the novel, as distinct from those who prefer the "old fashioned" idea of simply reading the book.

This is not the same as a radio adaptation, for there are no sound effects and only minimal music. It is a word for word rendering of the text, and it has to be said that it makes absorbing listening. Christopher Kay has a pleasant voice and makes the voices of the different characters sufficiently distinct. The effect is that of hearing a remarkable narrative confided to the listener by a friend. From the moment one hears the opening sentence — "Cigars had burned low, and we were beginning to sample the disillusionment that usually afflicts old school friends who meet again as men and find themselves with less in common than they used to think" — one is drawn irresistibly into Hilton's beguiling tale.

The *Lost Horizon* audiotapes are available from Soundings, Isis House, Kings Drive, Whitley Bay, NE26 2JT, U.K.

11

Lost Horizon
and the Modern World

Serious academic criticism of *Lost Horizon* did not get under way until after Hilton's death in 1954. Following the death of any writer there is inevitably a process of appraisal in which the author's work is reassessed and his or her enduring literary contribution is measured. In Hilton's case the process of reappraisal was slow to start but by the end of the twentieth century a number of important critical essays had been published, no fewer than three sequels had appeared, and work had begun on two major biographies.

Critical Essays

In an important essay published in 1962 Professor Harold C Martin of Harvard University drew attention to the two impulses that produce utopias — "discontent with the present and hope for a better future" — and went on to highlight Hilton's strengths as a story teller:

> Moreover, while Hilton may not be a great writer, he has a knack of making a story move. He draws his characters swiftly and with considerable humor. He knows how to exploit the mysterious and

how to keep a story taut with tension by placing clues adroitly with his left hand while the right goes on with the central narrative.[1]

Martin is surely right to underline Hilton's narrative skills. Before all else *Lost Horizon* is a *story* which makes the reader want to keep turning the pages to find out what happens next. However powerful or persuasive as a literary utopia, a polemic on world peace or an allegory on human nature the novel stands or falls by its strengths as a piece of storytelling. In drawing attention to this aspect Martin focuses on an aspect which is often overlooked in modern literary criticism: the ability of the novelist to hold the attention of the reader by framing a compelling narrative.

In the same essay Martin reminds us that "all fiction demands that we temporarily suspend our disbelief, that we agree to accept for the duration of the story whatever extraordinary situation or events the author chooses for his starting point."[2] By placing his story within the "frame" of a Prologue and an Epilogue, Martin argues, Hilton persuades us to accept the premises on which his narrative is based and temporarily suspend our skeptical faculties.

In his 1981 essay, "Utopian Eden of *Lost Horizon*," John W. Crawford compares and contrasts the utopias of H.G. Wells, the myth of the Garden of Eden, and the paradise of Shangri-La. After noting the differing approaches adopted by Wells and Hilton, Crawford concludes that in their separate ways:

> They provide both the basic stuff of life, and the satisfaction of the highest longings. Both utopias are literally unattainable; they are dreams.... But in their wake, they leave a feeling of hope, so that man is never entirely destitute. He is free to strive, and this alone helps to give meaning to life.[3]

Here Crawford highlights an important aspect of *Lost Horizon*—its significance from the point of view of satisfying human longings.

The novel has an honorable place in dream literature, and in this respect takes it place alongside Wells's short story, "The Door in the Wall," and Alain-Fournier's classic study of adolescent longing, *Le Grand Meaulnes* (usually translated into English under the title *The Lost Domain*).

Each of these posits a hidden, idyllic world which is found and then lost. Each has as its central character a hero who longs to rediscover an enchanted place he once glimpsed and cannot find again. Each is saturated with regret. John Fowles expresses this longing in these terms:

> They strive to maintain a constant state of yearning, they want eternally the mysterious house rising among the distant trees, eternally the footsteps through the secret gate, eternally the ravishingly beautiful and unknown girl beside the silent lake.[4]

James Hilton at the height of his fame. His novels *Lost Horizon, Goodbye Mr. Chips* and *Random Harvest* became best sellers on both sides of the Atlantic (courtesy the James Hilton Society).

The yearning to strive, to hope, to dream, is a basic human desire and in highlighting this aspect of the novel Crawford teases out one of its greatest strengths: that it appeals to the basic yearning for an unattainable place. Many readers will feel in their innermost hearts that Shangri-La is an impossible concept, that it cannot exist; at the same time there is the tantalizing thought that it *might just possibly exist.* It is this alluring thought which provides the inspiration for so much human endeavor.

The New Encyclopedia of Science Fiction edited by James Gunn and published in 1988 stated that *Lost Horizon* "may have been the last (and most successful) lost race novel."[5] In making this statement the author is reminding readers that the novel is one of a long line of lost race stories including the romances of S. Fowler Wright and Rider Haggard, and that a large part of its attraction lies in that fact. It is also a reminder that even today, despite greatly increased air travel and the Chinese occupation of

Tibet, the Karakoram and Kun Lun mountain ranges are one of the least explored areas of the world. Tibet as a source of lost civilization myths remains a potent and enduring symbol.

The fact that Tibet has been under Chinese occupation since 1950 might be thought to militate against the popular notion of that country as a lost paradise, but this does not seem to be the case. This is partly because vast tracts of the country are still inaccessible and only nominally under Chinese rule. The Kun Lun mountains, where Hilton located Shangri-La, remain to this day largely unexplored, though this vast mountain range contains peaks almost as high as Everest. The idea of Tibet as a source of mystery is so powerful and so firmly embedded in myths and legends that it is unlikely ever to be eradicated.

In a perceptive essay published in 1993 the science fiction writer Brian Stableford reviewed the significance of *Lost Horizon,* asserting that "There can be little doubt that *Lost Horizon* was a deeply personal book — every bit as intimately personal, in its own way, as *Goodbye Mr. Chips*." Stableford continues:

> In spite of their considerable differences at the surface level, Hilton's two most famous books have the same story buried within them, defining the structure of their emotional force. It is the story of a heart-sick man who miraculously finds his heart's desire in a most unexpected place, while far from home, and then proceeds to lose it again. The schoolmaster who loses his wife to unkind death has no means of literal recovery — even one as potentially hard-won as Conway's — but he does have the legacy of a personal transformation, which carries him forward regardless and grants him a kind of salvation.
>
> It is worth noting that *Random Harvest,* which is the story of another amnesiac hero, this time returned from the wars, who must learn to love his devoted wife all over again, is in essence the same story in yet another setting.[6]

Stableford is surely right to draw attention to the similarities between three of Hilton's most famous novels and to point out that all three are saturated with a sense of loss. Not until Robert Nathan's haunting tale *Portrait of Jennie,* published in 1940, do we find a comparable sense of longing.

The three novels for which Hilton is principally remembered today all have as their underlying theme the search for a lost happiness: *Lost Horizon* describes a search for the hidden idyll of Shangri-La, *Goodbye Mr. Chips* describes the love of a revered schoolmaster for an attractive and charismatic young woman, and *Random Harvest* tells the story of a successful public figure who is haunted by the memory of a happiness he once knew and strives to regain. In all three the central character is transformed by a life-enhancing experience which affects not only his own life but those around him and, significantly, the reader.

Stableford's essay merits close attention for it not only summarizes effectively the very real strengths of the novel but also urges careful study of the novel rather than the film, for "it is only in the pages of the original text that the true nature and depth of Conway's feelings is revealed and explored."

In *The Encyclopedia of Fantasy* (1997) two well known science fiction writers, John Clute and John Grant, drew attention to the significance of the novel as a seminal example of the literature of war. After stating that the Capra film version "changes some aspects but remains remarkably faithful in spirit to the book's marriage of cultural anxiety and escapist longing," Clute and Grant make an explicit link between the novel and the trauma of war:

> Conway, the protagonist, is a vicarious victim of World War One, a spiritually deadened Walking Wounded of a sort found quite frequently in novels of the 1920s; *Lost Horizon* itself is one of the last "aftermath" tales written, and perhaps the most resonant of all.[7]

In a reference work written at the very end of the twentieth century it is salutary to have this reminder of the novel's resonance, as an "aftermath" story bearing comparison with such works as Hemingway's *A Farewell to Arms* and Mann's *The Magic Mountain*. In highlighting the novel's significance from this perspective Clute and Grant underline the importance of *Lost Horizon* as an exemplar of war literature and as a novel of anxiety following one of the most destructive conflicts in history. Their appraisal neatly summarizes the essence of the book as a marriage between post war disillusionment and a yearning for a better life.

Finally came a tribute from a rather unlikely source: *The Rough Guide to Cult Fiction.* This volume — devoted to such cult figures as Albert Camus, J.G. Ballard, Ursula Le Guin and Damon Runyan — includes an interesting encomium of *Lost Horizon:*

> On one hand this is a sentimental, conservative novel in which the magical kingdom is an oasis of civilization. On the other, it anticipated the Zen, mystical strain in Western culture that saw many ... turn east in the 1960s seeking answers to life's conundrums....
> Hilton penned a thoughtful, upper-middlebrow novel that anticipated their quest.[8]

In a volume whose main aim is defined as "to introduce you to authors or novels that you might find intriguing, or to send you back to writers — and books — you already know for another look," it is encouraging to find an appraisal which looks beyond the novel as a piece of story telling and recognizes its deeper layers of meaning as a philosophical work. The same *Rough Guide* urges its readers to try Hilton's *Random Harvest* as "a novel of war and romance that prefigures *The English Patient.*" In this way a new generation of readers encountering Hilton for the first time may well be persuaded to delve deeper into his work and to discover for themselves its extraordinary appeal. Hilton could not have foreseen the "mystical strain in Western culture" which led many to question accepted values but he would surely have been gratified by his novel's continuing popularity in the 21st century.

Sequels

Hilton himself did not write a sequel to *Lost Horizon,* for reasons at which we can only guess. Presumably he felt he had said all he wanted to say. There can be no doubt that he continued to take a keen interest in his own creation, for he worked closely with Frank Capra and Robert Riskin on the 1937 film version, he was closely involved with numerous radio adaptations in the 1940s, and he also co-wrote some of the lyrics for the 1956 stage musical.

The first sequel to appear, *Return to Shangri-La* by Leslie Halliwell, was published in 1987. This is a highly readable and entertaining sequel, written by the well known film critic and author of numerous reference books on the cinema. The blurb tells us that the book was written as a tribute "to the magical adventure movies of the 1930s, a unique flight of fancy that will delight and entertain all those who admire his non-fiction works."

It tells the story of Nicholas Brent, a film producer who greatly admires Hilton's novel, becomes convinced that Shangri-La is a real place and sets out on a journey to find it. The book tells the story of his journey to Shangri-La, his success in reaching it and how an unscrupulous attempt to rob the lamasery of its gold is thwarted. For some reason Halliwell locates Shangri-La in the *south* of Tibet, not far from its frontier with Burma, whereas in the original novel Hilton locates it in the northwest of Tibet, somewhere in the Kun Lun mountains. Another incongruity which jarred on this reader is that at one point in the story a helicopter lands at the lamasery, which would surely have been impossible due to its inaccessibility. Much of the appeal of *Lost Horizon* lies in the reader's sense of *remoteness* of the community being described: to place it within reach of a helicopter destroys the illusion.

Apart from these minor blemishes, *Return to Shangri-La* can be recommended as a convincingly written sequel. The best sections of the book are a chapter purportedly written by Conway himself and describing events at Shangri-La during the years 1931–1940, and the final chapters describing the journey to the lamasery and Brent's meeting with Conway, Chang, Mallinson and Barnard. The book does not possess the charm and literary quality of *Lost Horizon*—that would be too much to expect—but it is a praiseworthy attempt to recapture the mood of Hilton's concept and as such is surely to be welcomed.

A further sequel, *Messenger* by Frank De Marco, appeared in 1994. The opening sequences are set in the year 1962 when an American U2 spy plane traveling on a secret military mission crashes in a remote part of Tibet. The pilot, George Chiari, survives and becomes a guest of Shangri-La. There he finds the Westerners described in Hilton's novel—Conway, Barnard and Miss Brinklow—and has many conversations with them. At first he wishes to leave the lamasery and even makes an unsuccessful attempt to escape, but eventually he is reconciled to his fate and decides to remain. He becomes more and more attuned to life at the lamasery and makes a determined effort to imbibe its philosophy. With the lapse of time he becomes a faithful disciple of Conway's and is content to enjoy Conway's friendship and the good humored company of his fellow countryman Barnard.

Seventeen years later, in 1979, another plane crashes nearby, the sole survivor being an American, Dennis Corbin, who had been working for the Chinese government. Conway realizes that with the Chinese occupation of Tibet Shangri-La can no longer count on remaining undiscovered, even though the lamasery is in a remote and inaccessible location. He decides that the best course will be to send a messenger to the outside world to help spread Shangri-La's philosophy of wisdom and peace. Chiari agrees to take on this role, partly because by this time he is anxious to re-open contact with his family and friends. With the help of the lamasery authorities he leaves Shangri-La and makes his way back to the Western world.

Messenger is an interesting story which seeks to bridge the gap between 1931, when the events in the original novel take place, and the time of the Chinese occupation. One of the most appealing aspects of the story is the description of lamasery inhabitants not mentioned by Hilton — including most notably Edith Bolton, known as "Sunnie," and an Englishman, Herrick — engaging characters one can imagine settling happily into life at Shangri-La. Like Halliwell's book it lacks the literary quality of *Lost Horizon* but it is certainly thought provoking and well merits careful reading as an attempt to translate Shangri-La's message to meet the needs of the modern world.

Yet another sequel, *Shangri-La* by Eleanor Cooney and Daniel Altieri, followed in 1996. This sequel was published in the United States by the long established firm of Morrow (publishers of the original American edition of *Lost Horizon*) but unfortunately it failed to find a British publisher. Cooney and Altieri are the authors of the acclaimed best sellers *Court of the Lion* and *Deception*, romances set in seventh and eighth century China.

Shangri-La is a much more "literary" production than Halliwell's novel, carefully and elegantly written. It is set in the year 1966, and describes an abortive attempt by General Zhang of the Chinese army to trace the location of Shangri-La and plunder it of its treasures. The authors have clearly studied *Lost Horizon* assiduously, and there are many allusions to Hilton's novel. Particularly memorable is a long section narrated by Conway, describing his experiences after leaving the lamasery with Mallinson and Lo Tsen in 1931. Conway goes on to describe his loss of memory, the gradual regaining of his memory following his meeting with the pianist Sieveking, his journey across Tibet in search of Shangri-La and his eventual success in finding the lamasery. The description of Shangri-La itself is particularly well done, as is the account of how Zhang's attempt to locate it is foiled by Conway's ingenuity.

The book succeeds very well in capturing the atmosphere of Hilton's novel: indeed, its subtitle is "The Return to the World of *Lost Horizon*." The book also vividly recalls the feeling of loss which affects the reader after closing the pages of the original novel; as Conway expresses it in this sequel: "It's an uneasy sense of loss, a feeling that something extraordinarily wonderful and extraordinarily sad has slipped away from me."[9]

Shangri-La is a worthy sequel to *Lost Horizon* and is a book to return to again and again. There are few modern novels of which this can be said.

Unanswered Questions

One of the reasons why so many writers have tried their hand at producing a sequel is that the original novel leaves a number of questions unresolved. For example, at the end of the story we are told that Lo-Tsen is with the porters "about five miles beyond the pass" (200). But it is not explained how Lo-Tsen, unaccompanied, could have crossed the traverse when Mallinson himself had found the same journey impossible without help.

A further difficulty is the question of Lo-Tsen's age. We are told that she was eighteen in 1884 and was therefore 65 in 1931 when the events in the story take place. The Chinese doctor described her as "most old of any one I have ever seen," which on the face of it seems unlikely. Cooney and Altieri in their sequel attempt to get round this difficulty by claiming that Lo-Tsen had lied about her true age and was in fact 80 rather than 65.[10]

These are characteristic of the kind of unresolved problems posed by the novel. Hilton is careful to point out that these questions might have been answered by Conway if he had had more time (227). As it is, we are left with a number of tantalizing riddles which continue to intrigue and will no doubt feature in sequels yet to be written.

Where Is Shangri-La?

As we approach the 75th anniversary of the publication of *Lost Horizon* attention is turning to the precise location of Shangri-La. In recent years numerous articles have been published claiming to have established the location of Hilton's lost paradise.

In 2002 two American mountaineers, Edward Vaill and Peter Klika, claimed to have pinpointed the exact location Hilton had had in mind when writing his novel. Vaill had spent twenty years researching Hilton's sources and was convinced that the ancient kingdom of Muli, an area between Doacheng, Zhongdian and Jiulong in the Sichuan province of China is the real Shangri-La. It is known that one of Hilton's sources was a series of articles in *National Geographic* magazine written by the eccentric American botanist and explorer Joseph Rock. Rock had described his extensive visits to the Sichuan province (then part of Tibet) including a beautiful mountain, Mount Jambejang, described as "a peaceful pyramid." Vaill and Klika became convinced that the lost kingdom of Muli, depicted so vividly by Rock, was Hilton's primary inspiration for Shangri-La. This conviction was strengthened when they interviewed Jane Wyatt, who had taken the part of Sondra in the Frank Capra film version and was the only surviving member of the 1937 cast. Jane Wyatt had met Hilton during the making of the film and Hilton had confided to her that the articles by Joseph Rock had been, at least in part, a primary source in his concept of the lost valley.

Vaill and Klika launched an expedition to Tibet and eventually found the kingdom of Muli but only after a hazardous journey, partly on horseback and partly on foot. The spot is so mountainous and hidden (even more remote than Hilton describes) that the few roads they found were often washed away by landslides. At the end of their journey they found what they described as "a magical place" with a lush valley, a monastery and a village inhabited by happy, peaceful folk.

The Chinese government, keen to capitalize on the Shangri-La legend, is investing considerable sums in building an airport and hotels in a remote mountainous region between Yunnan and Sichuan, but fortunately this spot is a considerable distance from the area identified by Vaill and Klika. The two mountaineers say they are not worried by the idea of Shangri-La as a tourist attraction as long as Muli and its people are left in peace. Vaill adds:

> The people who live there are very happy with their lives. The only tourists who visit there are Tibetan Buddhist pilgrims. Let other countries build their airports and hotels — but leave these people in peace.[11]

In 1989 Peter Bishop published his important study *The Myth of Shangri-La*. This is not so much a study of *Lost Horizon* as a detailed examination of the idea of a "sacred landscape" and the extraordinary appeal of Tibet for explorers and geographers over many centuries. Bishop states:

> Tibet seemed to offer hope, not just for a personal despair but for the malaise of an entire civilization, and perhaps for the whole world. James Hilton's *Lost Horizon*, first published in 1933, brilliantly encapsulated and popularized this symbolic drama.... Hilton's vision of Shangri-La joined Blavatsky's mahatmas and Kipling's lama in *Kim* as one of the great mythologizings about Tibet.[12]

Bishop's book is a major contribution to the serious study of utopian writings. Subtitled "Tibet, Travel Writing and the Western Creation of Sacred Landscape," *The Myth of Shangri-La* offers a comprehensive survey of the concept of a sacred place and the significance of Tibet within this myth. Charting the gradual discovery of Tibet by the Western world and the undying appeal of the notion of a hidden paradise, the book marks a milestone in the literary study of utopias. In surveying the whole subject in a scholarly and dispassionate manner Bishop fulfilled a valuable purpose, not least by demonstrating that the subject in itself merits serious academic scrutiny.

Michael McRae's *In Search of Shangri-La,* published in 2004, is subtitled "The extraordinary true story of the quest for the lost horizon." The book tells the story of Western attempts to uncover the mystery of the Tsangpo River, a sacred river according to Buddhist texts, for it supposedly leads to a paradisiacal hidden valley. According to McRae, the quest for this valley provided the inspiration for Hilton's novel and for Frank Capra's film. The book recounts the history of expeditions in search of the lost valley and the fabled waterfall believed to lead to it, neatly contrasting the notion of a sacred land as a place of pilgrimage and the quest as an end in itself or as a means of commercial exploitation.

Also in 2004 came Martin Brauen's lavishly illustrated work *Dreamworld Tibet* described as "a lively and visually engaging look at Western conceptions of Tibet." Ranging from 12th century myths to the legends of the lost kingdom of Shambhala, the book is a comprehensive survey of Western ideas of Tibet through the ages, demonstrating how our notions are colored by films, comics, novels and even advertising. *Dreamworld Tibet* provides an overview of conceptions of "the mystic East" from the work of occultists and explorers to popular films such as *Lost Horizon* and *Seven Years in Tibet.* The book acknowledges that *Lost Horizon* — both novel and film — has been a powerful influence in fostering the notion of Tibet as a hidden paradise but argues that this has tended to divert attention from the problems brought about by Chinese rule. "The Tibet Question," says Brauen, "will only be taken up in earnest when Tibet has been set free from Western fantasies and the myth of Shangri-La."[13]

Brauen does acknowledge, however that in writing *Lost Horizon* Hilton had skillfully drawn together a number of elements from legend and history — including Christian missionaries, gold deposits, the secret of longevity, seclusion and difficulty of access, an aged spiritual leader, a mysterious paradise — and woven these into a coherent and haunting narrative: "James Hilton made from the material a novel, a dreamlike modern fairy tale, which sold in several million copies."

Brauen is a respected figure in Tibetan studies (he is head of the Department of Tibet and Far East at the University of Zurich) and the author of several books in this field. His book is essential reading for anyone seeking to understand the historical and philosophical background to

Lost Horizon and is well worth perusing not only for its text but for its wealth of illustrations chosen from the worlds of art, cinema, legend and commerce.

To summarize, then, it is possible to identify the main lines of criticism of *Lost Horizon* that have emerged since Hilton's death in 1954:

- A study of the narrative as a contribution to the utopian tradition of Plato, More and Wells
- The novel as a case study in the art of the storyteller
- The novel as a variation on the theme of loss exemplified in *Goodbye Mr. Chips* and *Random Harvest*
- The novel as a work of fantasy in the tradition of Lewis and Tolkein
- The novel as an "unfinished" work which merits the writing of sequels to bring the story up to date
- The novel as an exemplar of the myth of the "sacred landscape" and the Tibetan utopia
- The novel as an example of the "aftermath" narrative emerging from the First World War
- A continuing fascination with the concept of Shangri-La as a real place

Optimistic or Pessimistic

A criticism frequently leveled at *Lost Horizon* is that Hilton "caught the mood of the time" but that things have moved on since then and the novel is now dated. For example, the website of Abebooks (Advanced Book Exchange) stated in 2002:

> Hilton was the right man for his time.... The bone-weary masses of the depression enthusiastically embraced the ideal "Shangri-La." Although Hilton's sentimentality, optimism and sense of melo-drama may now seem a bit old-fashioned, it still charms. Fantasy has become much darker in the post–nuclear age.[14]

It is worth examining this criticism as it expresses a widespread misconception regarding the novel. Is *Lost Horizon* an optimistic work? On the contrary, the thrust of the novel seems to the present writer to be deeply pessimistic. In the conversations between Conway and the High Lama the latter warns repeatedly of the dangers of world war and foresees terrible destruction in which all that is precious and lovely will be trampled to extinction. In stressing this vision the High Lama uses the words "war," "lust," "brutality," "destroy," "ruin," "storm," "desolation." The emphasis of his discourse is a reiterated warning of the imminent perils of war and the need to conserve the wisdom and heritage of the past:

> But the Dark Ages that are to come will cover the whole world in a single pall; there will be neither escape nor sanctuary, save such as are too secret to be found or too humble to be noticed [198].

Consider also the background to the events at Shangri-La. The journey to Tibet is preceded by violent revolution in Afghanistan accompanied by torture, rape and violence. It is followed (in the Epilogue) by bombing raids on China, with terrible civilian casualties — again emphasized by Hilton. Time and again we are reminded of man's savagery and duplicity. Far from being an optimistic work, the novel seems to me to be a salutary warning of the imminence of war and of the fragility of civilization. Conway's speculation that "Someday perhaps, the whole mountain would split, and a half of Karakal's icy splendor come toppling into the valley" (66) can be seen as a metaphor for the threat of destruction hanging over mankind. Hilton was surely right to stress the fragility of art, beauty and culture in the face of the rise of Fascism and Nazism and to plea for the conservation of civilized values. From this standpoint the novel can be seen as a timely warning of the dangers of world conflict. The statement that "Fantasy has become much darker in the post–nuclear age" is undoubtedly correct. The fantasies of J.R.R. Tolkein, C.S. Lewis, J.K. Rowling and Philip Pullman all have a dark element, but the reader should not be under any illusion that *Lost Horizon* is a work of cozy optimism.

Hilton's Literary Reputation

What is striking about *Lost Horizon* is the comparative lack of critical material. In sharp contrast to such authors as Orwell, Huxley and Wells

Lost Horizon has been the focus of comparatively little critical attention. Since Hilton's death there have been a number of school editions of the text and publishers which specialize in producing notes for students — Cliffs and Monarch in the United States and Coles in Britain — have issued background notes on the novel. Beyond this there is a marked paucity of critical matter. The reason for this seems to be a widely held perception that Hilton is not to be take seriously as a literary artist: that he was simply an entertainer. Typical of many comments is the following observation in Coles Notes:

> *Lost Horizon* is Hilton's best book. It is prophetic that as "Glory" Conway never fulfilled the promise of his early brilliance, so Hilton did not go on to write a great novel. He was content to turn out pleasant stories rather than serious works.[15]

And William Kenney in his Monarch Notes sums up the critical attitude towards the novel by saying: "The book ... is a very slight one but capable of giving its own very slight pleasure as long as one doesn't make the fatal mistake of taking it seriously."[16] The latest edition of the *Dictionary of National Biography,* published in 2004, sums up Hilton in similar vein by stating:

> Hilton was a professional middlebrow novelist ... to mid twentieth century readers and audiences the benevolent authority of Mr. Chips and the civilized serenity of Shangri-La offered escape, comforting entertainment and a fleeting reassurance of stability.[17]

Once again Hilton is pigeonholed as an escapist writer who offered his readers comforting entertainment but nothing more. The key words here are "middlebrow," "escape," "comfort" and "entertainment."

The present companion will, I hope, have demonstrated that Hilton is on the contrary an important writer who merits serious attention. As we enter the 21st century the time is overdue for a reappraisal of Hilton as a literary figure.

It is worth taking a closer look at the strange neglect which has apparently befallen Hilton and his works. He wrote three novels which were not only best sellers in their day but have stood the test of time: *Lost*

Horizon, Goodbye Mr. Chips and *Random Harvest*. He added the word "Shangri-La" to the English language and created a character, Mr. Chips, who has taken his place in the gallery of English characters alongside Wells's Mr. Polly and Arnold Bennett's Denry Machin. He made an important contribution to the Hollywood film industry, winning an Oscar for his work on the script of *Mrs. Miniver*. No fewer that eight of his novels have been adapted for the screen.

Despite all this it seems to have become his fate to have fallen into a kind of limbo. Though most people have heard of "Mr. Chips" and "Shangri-La" most readers would find difficulty in recalling the name of the author. I have even found quite literate people who claim never to have heard the name James Hilton at all. How are we to account for this neglect? The usual arguments put forward to account for this are that Hilton is out of fashion because he was a "sentimental" writer, and that his novels were written purely for entertainment, with no pretence of artistry or literary merit. Do these arguments hold water?

In Hilton's own view sentiment is precisely the quality which is missing from so many modern novels. If one defines sentiment as "a thought or body of thought, tinged with emotion" (*Chambers Twentieth Century Dictionary*) is this really something to be deplored? Are not *David Copperfield, The Mill on the Floss, The Old Wives' Tale* and *The Forsyte Saga* great novels precisely because they are animated by sentiment — that is to say, they are animated by the normal human qualities of affection, longing, regret, sympathy and love. A novel without sentiment would be a cold novel indeed.

Hilton himself observed:

> I don't mind being called a sentimentalist so long as it is not used in a derogatory sense. A lot of modern books have come out of the icebox and not out of the oven. They are cold cerebration.... All great novels of the world have been sentimental.[18]

One of the reasons why *Random Harvest* and *Goodbye Mr. Chips* were such highly successful novels (and films) is because they are "sentimental" in the sense that they deal with human emotions: happiness, grief, love, tenderness, affection, longing, loss and contentment. Are these not the substance of all great novels? One reason why the great films of the 1940s—for example *Random Harvest, And Now Voyager* and *Brief Encounter*—are so satisfying to watch today is because they deal with fundamental emotions and values in a way which contemporary films and novels do not.

The second charge, that Hilton was a lightweight novelist whose books bear no relation to literature, is one which is still sometimes heard and is perhaps worth a closer look.

The British critic A.C. Ward was typical of many when he wrote:

> For some years Hilton's main contribution to literature seemed to be *Lost Horizon,* its *dolce far niente* land of Shangri-La creating restful longings in its many thousands of readers and providing them with a simple philosophy distilled in persuasive prose.[19]

(It should be noted incidentally that this reveals a complete misreading of *Lost Horizon: dolce far niente* means "pleasant, idleness, total relaxation," which is certainly *not* the philosophy of Shangri-La.) Similarly the American critic William Kenney commented: "James Hilton is an example of 'popular' rather than 'serious' writer of fiction — that is, his appeal has been not to the selective few but to the less demanding many."[20]

The implication of both these criticisms is that Hilton was writing purely for entertainment. It is true that some of his early novels — *The Passionate Year,* for example — are of doubtful merit and suffer from being overmelodramatic (he was, after all, a young man still learning his craft) but it is difficult to see how this accusation can be sustained when considering the whole range of Hilton's work. Consider the conversations between Conway and the High Lama in *Lost Horizon,* the skilful manner in which Charles Rainier's personality is unfolded in *Random Harvest,* the evocative depiction of a Lancashire mill town in *So Well Remembered,* the vivid description of first love in *Time and Time Again.* Each of these novels merits careful reading to reveal its full literary quality: each merits reading not only once but a second or third time to bring out the nuances of its meanings.

The history of the English novel in the twentieth century is littered with best sellers which sold in enormous quantities in their day: one thinks of such titles as *The Green Hat* by Michael Arlen, *Sorrel and Son* by Warwick Deeping, *The Constant Nymph* by Margaret Kennedy or *The Rosary* by Florence Barclay. Where are they now? They have simply faded into obscurity. This fate has not overtaken *Lost Horizon, Goodbye Mr. Chips* and *Random Harvest,* which have been in print for seventy years and more. They would simply not have survived if they possessed no literary merit. They have survived because readers find in them qualities of enduring value, and because they witness to fundamental human truths.

The fact remains that, despite the popularity of some of his work, Hilton himself remains a shadowy figure and the bulk of his output remains little known. Whereas his contemporaries Graham Greene and George Orwell have had biographies and critical studies written about them, Hilton has received comparatively little critical attention. In many reference works on English Literature there are full entries for Graham Greene, Evelyn Waugh and H.E. Bates but often no entry at all for Hilton. Why is this? What qualities do the novels of Greene, Waugh and Bates possess which those by Hilton do not?

Literary fashions change with alarming rapidity. It does seem to be the case that the novels of Hilton and his contemporaries — Howard Spring, A.J. Cronin, Francis Brett Young, Dorothy Whipple — are temporarily out of fashion. The British writer and critic Richard Church commented perceptively:

> It is not often that the gentle writer, the advocate of quietness and sweetness of disposition, is quickly recognized. The tendency today is all for strong meat, especially in fiction.[21]

Church was writing in 1943 when the work of "gentle" writers such as Hilton was appreciated. But today the tendency is undoubtedly for "strong meat," with the virtues exemplified in Hilton's novels — gentleness, quietness, courtesy, compassion — out of favor. When Dorothy Whipple's novel *Someone at a Distance* (1953) failed to attract a single major review her publisher wrote to her saying, "Editors have gone mad about action and passion."[22] It may well be the case that "action and passion" are in favor at the moment and that for this reason Hilton's work has been temporarily eclipsed.

Paradoxically it is arguable that Hilton's reputation has suffered precisely because he was at one time so popular. In 1934 *Lost Horizon* and *Goodbye Mr. Chips* were both best-selling titles, particularly in the United States, and his name became a household word. When *Random Harvest* was published in 1941 it sold 100,000 copies in the first six weeks of publication and went through 22 printings in three years. These figures sound modest today when compared with the sales of *The Da Vinci Code* or the Harry Potter books by J.K. Rowling, but by the standards of that time these sales were phenomenal. In his hey day he was a runaway best-seller.

There persists a widely held view that because a novel is a "best seller" it cannot therefore be regarded as literature. Daphne du Maurier's *Rebecca* and Margaret Mitchell's *Gone with the Wind* were both frowned on in academic circles because they enjoyed a wide popular readership. In this sense Hilton has been the victim of his own success. The real strengths of his novels have tended to be overlooked because he has been pigeonholed as a popular, "low-brow" novelist whose works do not merit serious study. F. Scott Fitzgerald, John Steinbeck, Ernest Hemingway, George Orwell and Aldous Huxley have all attracted considerable critical attention in recent years but Hilton has been largely bypassed by the academic world. This is evident from the fact that many reference works do not mention Hilton at all. For example, the *Concise Cambridge Bibliography of English Literature* edited by George Watson (Cambridge University Press, 1966) and *A Guide to English and American Literature* by F.W. Bateson and H.T. Meserole (Longman, 1976) completely ignore Hilton. Do we infer from this that Hilton is not part of English Literature?

To a large degree the question of which works of fiction are regarded as meriting serious academic scrutiny is arbitrary. In his critical study *Unlocking the Text: Fundamental Issues in Literary Theory* Jeremy Hawthorn writes:

> It should be noted that inclusion in the canon was normally argued in *de facto* terms: if most university departments of literature agreed that certain works merited serious study, then these works were, *ipso facto*, canonical. Subsequent explanations of the merit of

these works might be ventured, but no abstract definition of what qualified a work for canonization could normally be found.[23]

Seen in this light it is apparent that there is no obvious reason why *Lost Horizon* is not regarded as a work of literature: it is simply a matter of fashion and prevailing taste. The fact remains that *Lost Horizon* is one of those novels which has stood the test of time. Had it not been well written it would simply have faded into oblivion and suffered the same fate as the works of Marie Corelli and Dornford Yates. It is also worth remembering that fashions in reading fluctuate, just as fashions change in music, art and painting. Hilton's novels are temporarily in eclipse but this situation could well change.

Meanwhile there are now real signs of a gradual renewal of interest in Hilton. In the year 2000 a James Hilton Society was established to promote interest in his life and work. This soon began a regular program of meetings and publications, and has already held conferences on the major novels and films including *Lost Horizon, Random Harvest* and *Goodbye Mr. Chips*. A Canadian publisher, George Vanderburgh, has commenced an ambitious program of reissuing some of the long out of print novels including *Storm Passage, The Silver Flame* and *Terry*.

Plaques have now been placed on the houses where Hilton lived and worked including, significantly, the house on Oak Hill Gardens, Woodford Green, Essex, where *Lost Horizon* was written. This plaque was erected by English Heritage, the body responsible for the famous Blue Plaques on the houses of literary and cultural figures. A press report at the time stated:

> Oak Hill Gardens, a quiet cul de sac backing on the Epping Forest, was packed with onlookers as the prized English Heritage blue plaque was unveiled at number 42. Its name is Shangri-La, once the most popular house name in Britain. But this is probably the only property in the world truly entitled to use it, for it was here that James Hilton created the magic land.[24]

Two major biographies of Hilton are currently being written: one by the American critic Frederick Ott, and one by the British writer Timothy Carroll. This is a significant development for the publication of a

The plaque at Leigh, Lancashire (Hilton's birthplace), commemorating his life and work (courtesy the James Hilton Society).

biography is in itself an indication of a writer's importance and sets in train a process of criticism and reappraisal. This in turn necessitates a closer look at Hilton's life and achievement including a reassessment of his novels and films. Indeed, bearing in mind Hilton's former fame it is surprising that a full-scale biography of him has not been attempted before.

Information regarding his life is hard to come by for he left no autobiography apart from a "Chapter of Autobiography" in his volume of short stories *To You Mr. Chips* (1938), which only concerns his school years and is in any case lacking in detail. He was a reticent man who preferred to live quietly away from the media spotlight.

We come back to the extraordinary resilience of *Lost Horizon* which, alone of his twenty novels, seems to go from strength to strength, H.G. Wells once wrote: "Things written either live or die ... there is no apologetic intermediate state."[25] How true that is.

Given the fact that Hilton himself is out of fashion and that the bulk of his novels are out of print, how do we account for the continuing popularity of this one novel? There is, first, the point that the novel is a supreme example of the Tibetan utopia. The fact that Tibet has been under Chinese rule since 1950 has not diminished its appeal nor lessened the potency of Tibet as a land of mystery and legend. Novels depicting a hidden paradise have always been popular, hence the extraordinary appeal of such works as Edward Bellamy's *Looking Backward* and B.F. Skinner's *Walden Two*. The unique appeal of *Lost Horizon* lies in the fact that it depicts a world just beyond our reach, a land that is attractive and possible and yet seemingly unattainable. The idea that it is *there*, waiting for us and just over the horizon is a powerful element in its appeal. It is a novel told with extraordinary conviction: while reading it one has the illusion that this is not a work of fiction but an account written by an eyewitness who has seen Shangri-La for himself.

Lost Horizon has taken its place alongside other twentieth century classics such as Daphne du Maurier's *Rebecca* (1938) and George Orwell's *Nineteen Eighty Four* (1949) as one of those works which caught the mood of the generation and expressed the hopes and fears of a multitude of readers. One has only to read the opening sentence — "Cigars had burned low, and we were beginning to sample the disillusionment that usually afflicts old school friends who meet again as men and find themselves with less in common than they used to think"—to be immediately transported back to a world which now has a certain period charm: a world redolent of the short stories of Maugham and Wells. It is a mood in which the reader knows that a *story* is about to be unfolded, one which will hold the attention to the final page and which will be *absorbing*.

A further reason for its continuing popularity is that it appeals to readers of many different persuasions. It is a tale of *adventure*, telling a gripping story of a journey across unexplored mountains culminating in the discovery of a lost valley. It is a *romance*, describing the love story between Conway and Lo-Tsen and its tragic aftermath. It is a *utopia*, following in the tradition of Samuel Butler's *Erewhon* and Aldous Huxley's *Island*. It is a *quest* narrative, recalling the romances of Rider Haggard and the Arthurian legends of the search for the Holy Grail. In addition to all these elements it is a story of *regret*, leaving the reader with a sense of irreparable loss and yearning. It is above all a novel with a *philosophical* dimension, a story which is designed to stimulate thought by posing fundamental questions concerning the human predicament and the nature of happiness.

We should not underestimate the appeal of Conway himself. He is an attractive, charismatic character who appeals to many different readers because he is both a man of action and a man of ideas. As a man of action he is capable of decisive leadership and is especially skilful at times of crisis. He is a natural leader, bringing out the best in his subordinates and remaining calm at times of stress. As a man of ideas he is wise beyond his years, able to converse with the High Lama on philosophy and history and appreciate all that is good in the legacy of East and West. Above all he is a man who is most at home in the world of thought, wisdom and contemplation, a man who loves quietness and for that reason finds Shangri-La deeply appealing. The fact that Conway's personality is unfolded to the reader in gradual stages adds to his enigmatic quality. The unsolved mystery surrounding him also adds to his appeal. What happens to Conway in the end? Does he succeed in finding his way back to Shangri-La? The tantalizing element of doubt lingers in the mind long after the last page has been reached.

Unlike many much hyped "best sellers," which are by their very nature transitory, *Lost Horizon* has continued to be read and enjoyed for seventy years and more. In the "Narrative Art" section we drew attention to its literary and imaginative qualities and to its skilful use of language. It is a well written novel, told in a fluent, economical style in prose of arresting quality. Some of the images from the narrative have become indelibly fixed in the mind — the first encounter with Chang in his hooded chair, the first glimpse of Shangri-La, the meeting with the High Lama, the appearance of Lo-Tsen, Conway's succession and the High Lama's death, the flight from the lamasery. These images (reinforced by film versions and radio adaptations) remain in the forefront of the imagination with such clarity that it is as if we have witnessed them ourselves.

It is clear from the above that *Lost Horizon* has achieved the status of a modern classic. It is a novel that will bear reading and re-reading, which will repay careful study, and will reveal new layers of meaning with each perusal. When the young James Hilton — then a little known journalist living from hand to mouth — sat down to write his novel in the spring of 1933 he could have had no inkling that he was producing a work that would carry his name and reputation into the next century.

Appendix 1

Questions for Discussion

Prologue

1. Why does Hilton begin his novel with a Prologue instead of launching directly into the story?

2. What does Rutherford mean when he states that Wyland has "the complete head-prefectorial mind?" Is this criticism justified?

3. Discuss the attitudes of Rutherford, Wyland and the narrator toward Conway. Why are their perceptions of Conway so different?

4. What have the three Englishmen in common?

Chapter 1

1. If you had been one of the passengers in the hijacked plane how would you have reacted?

2. Discuss the differences in the reactions of (a) Conway, (b) Mallinson and (c) Barnard. Which reaction seems to you to be the most sensible? Why?

Chapter 2

1. We are told that Conway disapproved of the Western ideal of superlatives in sport and achievement. Why was this?

2. What does Miss Brinklow mean by saying the arrival of Chang and his party is providential?

Chapter 3

1. "Part of Conway was always an onlooker, however active might be the rest." What does this statement mean?
2. Why do the Tibetans allow Conway to deputize while Chang is asleep during the journey?

Chapter 4

1. What does Conway mean when he states that a separate culture might flourish at Shangri-La without "contamination" from the world outside?
2. Mallinson and Conway appear to have totally different attitudes toward the pace of life. How would you define their differences?

Chapter 5

1. What is it about Shangri-La that Conway finds attractive? Do the others share his enthusiasm?
2. Why does Conway decide not to tell his companions about his discovery that they have been deliberately brought to Shangri-La?

Chapter 6

1. What does Conway mean by telling Chang that he is geared differently? What is different about Chang's attitude to time?
2. What is the basis of law and order at Shangri-La?
3. Is an ideal community of this kind practicable?

Chapter 7

1. Why was Henschell's contribution to the development of Shangri-La so important?

2. What is the proviso governing Shangri-La's reception of guests? Why is this proviso necessary?

Chapter 8

1. What is the High Lama's vision of the future? To what extent has his forecast proved to be accurate?

2. What is the quality about Conway which the High Lama finds interesting and unusual?

Chapter 9

1. Why does Mallinson feel that the situation in Baskul was healthier than that at Shangri-La?

2. Discuss the respective attitudes of Chang and Conway toward the word "slacker."

Chapter 10

1. What are the reasons why Conway, Barnard and Miss Brinklow all wish to remain at Shangri-La?

2. Why does the High Lama decide to appoint Conway as his successor?

Chapter 11

1. "At the mention of Lo-Tsen the two worlds touched and fused suddenly in Conway's mind." What does this statement mean?

2. Why did Mallinson not simply remain at Shangri-La with Lo-Tsen?

3. Do you approve or disapprove of Conway's decision to leave Shangri-La? Why?

Epilogue

1. Why does Rutherford state that Conway's narrative is "an exercise in the balancing of probabilities?"

2. In what ways was Conway changed by his experiences during the First World War?

3. What do you think happened to Mallinson and Lo-Tsen?

Appendix 2

Hilton's Preface
to *Lost Horizon*

Lost Horizon was first published on both sides of the Atlantic in the autumn of 1933. Its sale was slow at first, and though it had a few fervent and even notable admirers, by Christmas of that year one might have prophesied that even the ripple it had stirred was already stilled. As this happens to ninety-nine percent of novels, I was not enormously surprised, though I was — dare I now say it? — a little disappointed. But in June 1934, the story received the Hawthornden Prize, which is given yearly in England for an imaginative work written by a British author under the age of forty-one. The result was in the nature of a resurrection; the sale of the original English edition began to gather momentum, while in America the publishers took the almost unique step of issuing the book afresh. Such a second chance was well taken, for during the past two years seventeen editions have been printed. This, the eighteenth, makes a permanent one.

I recount these details without vainglory, though I cannot pretend to be indifferent over them. There is certainly no book of mine whose success I ever desired more keenly, for *Lost Horizon* was, in part, the expression of a mood for which I had always hoped to find sympathizers. I found them in thousands, and now, through the medium of the screen version that Frank Capra has made, the same mood, I hope, will find them in millions.

Which leads me to a final remark about this mood. When *Lost Horizon* first appeared three years ago, its message of the peril of war to all that we mean by the word "civilization" was considered topical.

It will be such a storm as the world has not seen before. There will be no safety by arms, no help from authority, no answer in science. It will rage till every flower of culture is trampled, and all human things are leveled in a vast chaos ... the Dark Ages that are to come will cover the whole world in a single pall; there will be neither escape nor sanctuary, save such as are too secret to be found or too humble to be noticed.

How much happier one would be to dismiss all this as thoroughly out-of-date, than to admit, as one must, that in 1936 it has become more terrifyingly up-to-date than ever!

James Hilton
London, August 4, 1936

Appendix 3

The James Hilton Circle

Balgarnie, William (1869–1951), schoolmaster. Known affectionately to generations of pupils as "Uncle," Balgarnie was classics master at The Leys School, Cambridge from 1900 to 1929 and again from 1939 to 1946. He became a Leysion institution and an authority on all matters relating to the school. The character of Mr. Chipping in Hilton's story *Goodbye Mr. Chips* was based in part on Balgarnie, and in part on Hilton's own father, John Hilton. After his death *The Times* obituary stated: "Balgarnie had become so closely identified with the school and all its interests that his passing will seem to mark the end of an epoch in its history."

Brown, Alice Helen (1903–1962), first wife of James Hilton. After working as a secretary at the British Broadcasting Corporation she married Hilton at Eastbourne Register Office on 19 October 1935, shortly before sailing to the United States. They divorced in 1937 but were later reconciled. She remained his companion until his death in 1954 and nursed him in his final illness, after which she became his literary executor. They are buried in adjacent graves at Knollkreg Memorial Park, Abingdon, Virginia.

Burnham, Barbara playwright and producer. She joined the BBC Drama Department in 1933 as a play adaptor, and produced and adapted radio plays until 1945. In 1938 she collaborated with Hilton in writing a three-act play based on *Goodbye Mr. Chips*. Later she became a television producer. She and Hilton remained friends and in 1943 he sent her an inscribed copy of *The Story of Dr. Wassell*.

Capra, Frank (1897–1991), film director. Capra was responsible for some major films including *It Happened One Night* (1934), *Mr. Deeds Goes to Town*

(1936), *Arsenic and Old Lace* (1944) and *It's a Wonderful Life* (1946). He directed the classic 1937 film version of *Lost Horizon* and purchased Hilton's original manuscript from a London bookdealer.

Colman, Ronald (1891–1958), actor. Following military service in the First World War and several years' stage experience in Britain, Colman went to Hollywood in 1920 and appeared in a number of silent films before making the transition to sound in *Bulldog Drummond* (1929). He starred in some distinguished movies including *A Tale of Two Cities* (1936), *The Prisoner of Zenda* (1937), *Random Harvest* (1942), *The Late George Apley* (1947) and *A Double Life* (1948). He is particularly remembered for his portrayal of Conway in Frank Capra's adaptation of *Lost Horizon,* and for his performance as Rainier in the film version of *Random Harvest.* Colman, Greer Carson and Hilton were all members of the English "colony" in Hollywood.

Cronin, A.J. (Archibald Joseph) (1896–1981), novelist. After serving for some years as a doctor in Wales and London, Cronin achieved fame as a novelist. He was the author of *Hatter's Castle* (1931), *The Stars Look Down* (1935), *The Citadel* (1937), *The Keys of the Kingdom* (1941), and other best-selling works. To the amusement of both men Hilton was mistakenly regarded by some as the author of *The Citadel* and Cronin was mistakenly identified as the author of *Goodbye Mr. Chips.*

Cutts, Leonard editor. As editor of the *British Weekly,* a leading Nonconformist journal, in November 1933 Cutts invited Hilton to write a 3,000 word short story for the Christmas issue of the paper. The story became *Goodbye Mr. Chips,* written in four days. This was later published in book form and became extremely popular, stimulating the sales of *Lost Horizon.* Hilton and Cutts remained lifelong friends. In 1969 he wrote the Foreword to a new edition of *Goodbye Mr. Chips* in which he paid a warm tribute to Hilton.

Dickson, Lovat (1902–1987), writer and editor. Dickson began his working life as the editor of a weekly newspaper in Canada, and later became editor of the London *Fortnightly Review.* He then joined the staff of the publishing house Macmillan, who were closely associated with Hilton, and was a director from 1941 until 1964. His works include *The Ante-Room* (1960), *The House of Words* (1963) and *H.G. Wells: His Turbulent Life and Times* (1969). As a friend of Hilton's Dickson contributed the entry on him in the *Dictionary of National Biography,* observing that Hilton had "a talent for evoking the finer feelings in his readers, for making people feel better about other people, and for underscoring the praiseworthy virtues."

Donat, Robert (1905–1958), actor. After years of experience on the stage Donat starred in a number of films including *The Count of Monte Cristo* (1934) and *The Thirty Nine Steps* (1935) and starred opposite Marlene Dietrich in the film version of Hilton's novel *Knight without Armour* (1937). He won an Academy Award for his portrayal of Mr. Chipping in the film version of *Goodbye Mr. Chips* (1939) and received a warm letter of congratulations from Hilton. Earlier Donat had sought Hilton's advice on the portrayal.

Franklin, Sidney   (1893–1972), film producer. One of the most distinguished American producer-directors, Franklin's film credits included *The Barretts of Wimpole Street* and *The Good Earth*. He was closely involved with four of Hilton's films: *Goodbye Mr. Chips, Mrs. Miniver, Random Harvest* and *Madame Curie*. Michael Troyan in his biography of Greer Garson, *A Rose for Mrs. Miniver,* described Franklin as "a consummate artist, and consequently one of the most admired and respected men at Metro Goldwyn Mayer."

Froeschel, George   scriptwriter. Froeschel usually worked as a member of a scriptwriting team including Arthur Wimperis and Claudine West. He co-wrote the scripts for a number of Hilton's films including *Mrs. Miniver* and *Random Harvest.* He also contributed to the scripts of numerous films of the 1940s including *Waterloo Bridge* and *The White Cliffs of Dover.*

Garson, Greer   (1904–1996), actress. Following several years stage experience in Britain, Garson was invited to Hollywood in 1937 and was later cast as Mrs. Chipping in the film version of *Goodbye Mr. Chips,* (1939). She starred in some of the major films of the 1940s including *Pride and Prejudice* (1940), *Mrs. Miniver* (1942), *Random Harvest* (1942), *Madame Curie* (1943) and *The Forsyte Saga* (1949). She and Hilton became close friends. Two of her films — *Goodbye Mr. Chips* and *Random Harvest*—were based on novels by him; a third, *Mrs. Miniver,* was largely written by him, and a fourth, *Madame Curie,* was narrated by him. They also had in common the fact that they were both English but had settled in Hollywood.

Hilton, Elizabeth   formerly Burch (1870–1943), mother of James Hilton. After working as a schoolteacher Elizabeth married John Hilton in 1898 and gave birth to her only child, James, in September 1900, at Leigh, Lancashire, the town of her birth. Shortly afterward John and Elizabeth returned to Walthamstow, London, where John was a schoolmaster. They joined James in California during the war years but she died there in 1943.

Hilton, John   (1871–1955), father of James Hilton. He began teaching at Forest Road School, Walthamstow, in 1895 and in 1898 married Elizabeth Burch, who was also a schoolteacher. Their only son, James, was born in September 1900. In 1902 he became headmaster of Chapel End Junior Mixed School, Walthamstow, where he remained until 1932. In 1921 he and his wife

Elizabeth went to live at "Leigh," Oak Hill Gardens, Woodford Green, Essex, where James joined them after completing his studies at Cambridge. *Lost Horizon* was written in this house. John Hilton lived with James in California during the Second World War and returned to England when the war was over. He died in October 1955.

Kopineck, Galina   Hilton's second wife. Formerly an actress married to the concert pianist Max Rabinowitz, she married Hilton in April 1937, seven days after his divorce from Alice Brown. She lived with Hilton for some years but divorced him in 1945. After his death Galina did not share in the estate as he had paid her a lump sum as a financial settlement.

Le Roy, Mervyn   (1900–1987), film director and producer. One of the most accomplished and versatile directors of his time, LeRoy directed numerous films including *Waterloo Bridge* (1940), *Blossoms in the Dust* (1941), *Madame Curie* (1943), *Little Women* (1949), and *Quo Vadis* (1951). He is particularly remembered for the film adaptation of *Random Harvest* (1942), which was nominated for seven Academy Awards and is now regarded as a classic of its kind. Hilton spoke the opening narration.

Macmillan, Daniel   (1886–1965), publisher. A classical scholar, Macmillan joined the board of the publishing house at the age of 25 and was chairman from the death of Sir Frederick Macmillan in 1936 until his own death in 1965. He was the brother of Harold Macmillan, British prime minister from 1957 to 1963. Daniel gave encouragement to Hilton when *Lost Horizon* was published and was present at the ceremony when the Hawthornden Prize was awarded to Hilton in 1934. Hilton's novels continued to be published under the Macmillan imprint throughout the remainder of his literary career.

Marion, Frances   (1890–1973), scriptwriter. One of the leading American screenwriters, she wrote the scripts of a number of distinguished films including *The Scarlet Letter* (1927), *The Big House* (1930), *The Champ* (1932) and *Dinner at Eight* (1933). She worked with Hilton on the screenplay of *Camille* (1936) and also contributed to the script of his novel *Knight without Armour* (1937). She and Hilton became close friends. In a 1937 article about Hollywood, "The Maligned Village," Hilton described her as "the most generous person alive."

Paxton, John   (born 1911), American screenwriter. Paxton was responsible for some highly literate film scripts including *Farewell My Lovely* (1943), *Crossfire* (1947) and *Fourteen Hours* (1951). In 1947 he wrote the script for the film version of Hilton's novel *So Well Remembered*, which was filmed in England and narrated by Hilton.

Riskin, Robert   (1897–1955), screenwriter. One of the most distinguished American scriptwriters, Riskin was responsible for the screenplays of numerous films including *It Happened One Night* (1934), *Mr. Deeds Goes to Town* (1936), *The Real Glory* (1939) and *Meet John Doe* (1941). He wrote the script for Frank Capra's version of *Lost Horizon,* on which Hilton was consulted.

Roberts, Cecil   (1892–1976), novelist and playwright. The author of many books including *Victoria Four-Thirty* (1937) and *Pilgrim Cottage* (1933), Roberts became a close friend of Hilton, describing him as "a man who imparted his gift of enjoyment with a modesty and warmth that never deserted him."

Saville, Victor   (1897–1979), British film producer and director. Saville was responsible for some of the outstanding movies of the 1930s including *The Good Companions* (1932), *South Riding* (1938) and *The Citadel* (1938). As the producer of *Goodbye Mr. Chips* he worked closely with Hilton and the director Sam Wood on the casting of the film. It was their inspired choice of Greer Garson to play the part of Katherine Chipping which launched Garson on her long Hollywood career. Saville was also closely involved with the Anglo-American production *Forever and a Day* (1943) — the history of a London house from 1804 to 1940, and Hilton contributed to the script.

Sherriff, Robert Cedric   (1896–1975), author and screenwriter. Mainly remembered today as the author of the play *Journey's End* (1928), Sherriff contributed to numerous films including *That Hamilton Woman* (1941) and *The Night My Number Came Up* (1955). He made an important contribution to two of Hilton's films *Goodbye Mr. Chips* (1939) and *Mrs. Miniver* (1942), and wrote the Dunkirk sequence for *Mrs. Miniver.*

Smith, C. Aubrey   (1863–1948), actor. A distinguished British actor in Hollywood for many years, Aubrey Smith starred in numerous epic films including *The Prisoner of Zenda* (1937), *The Four Feathers* (1939), *Rebecca* (1940), *Madame Curie* (1943) and *An Ideal Husband* (1947). Together with Ronald Colman, Greer Garson, and Hilton himself, he was a leading member of the British "colony" in Hollywood. At the memorial service following his death Hilton paid warm tribute to him, praising his qualities of Englishness and steadfastness.

Squire, Sir John   (1884–1958), critic, editor and poet. John Collings Squire became literary editor of the *New Statesman* and founded the *London Mercury* in 1919, one of the leading literary journals of its time. He was an important influence in the literary world and was the author of several collections of poetry, criticism and short stories. He was the leading figure in a group of poets and critics which detractors referred to as "the Squirearchy," notable for their dislike of "avant-garde" writers. It was Squire who recommended that

Macmillan publish *Lost Horizon* and was thus responsible for Hilton's long connection with this publishing house.

Thalberg, Irving   (1899–1936), film production executive. Following experience as head of Universal Studios, Thalberg became production supervisor of MGM in 1924. He was responsible for some of the major films of the 1930s including *The Barretts of Wimpole Street* (1934), *Mutiny on the Bounty* (1935) and *Romeo and Juliet* (1936). He invited Hilton to come to Hollywood in 1936 to assist in writing scripts for film adaptations of his novels. Thalberg was known as the "boy genius" of Hollywood and was satirized in Scott Fitzgerald's novel *The Last Tycoon* (1941).

West, Claudine   scriptwriter. West usually worked as a member of a scriptwriting team including George Froeschel and Arthur Wimperis. She co-wrote the scripts for a number of Hilton's films including *Goodbye Mr. Chips*, *Mrs. Miniver* and *Random Harvest*.

Wimperis, Arthur   (1874–1953), screenwriter. One of the most prolific British librettists and scriptwriters, Wimperis was educated at University College, London, and contributed to many, British films including Hilton's *Knight without Armour* (1937) and *The Four Feathers* (1939). Later moving to Hollywood, he made notable contributions to *Mrs. Miniver* and *Random Harvest*, receiving an Academy Award for his work on the script of *Mrs. Miniver*.

Wood, Sam   (1883–1949), film director. Wood directed many memorable films including *A Night at the Opera* (1935), *Raffles* (1939) and *Kitty Foyle* (1940). He directed the classic film version of *Goodbye Mr. Chips* (1939) starring Robert Donat and Greer Garson. In later years Wood and Hilton disagreed strongly as Hilton was a moderate liberal in the Hollywood of the McCarthy era whereas Wood strongly backed McCarthy.

Woollcott, Alexander   (1887–1943), writer and critic. As the *New York Times* theatre critic from 1914 to 1922 Woollcott was an influential literary figure and hosted the radio program *Town Crier* from 1929 to 1942. In 1934 he devoted an entire episode to *Goodbye Mr. Chips,* proclaiming it 'the most profoundly moving story that has passed this way in several years," and was thus instrumental in launching Hilton's career in the United States.

Appendix 4

A *Lost Horizon* Chronology

1933   *Lost Horizon* is published simultaneously by Macmillan, London, and William Morrow, New York

1934   Hilton is awarded the Hawthornden Prize. Publication of the "Hawthornden Prize Edition" by William Morrow

1936   Publication of the Author's Edition by William Morrow, containing a specially written Preface by Hilton

1937   Film version by Columbia Pictures Corporation, starring Ronald Colman, Jane Wyatt and H.B. Warner

1939   First paperback edition published by Pocket Books, New York

1943   Translated into French

1944   Translated into Spanish

1947   First British paperback edition published by Pan Books, London

1950   Translated into Japanese

1954   Death of James Hilton

1956   Musical version, *Shangri-La*, opens on Broadway

1966   Pan Books, London, reprints the novel for the 9th time, marking the publication of 400,000 copies in Pan paperback editions

1969   Pocket Books, New York, reprints the novel for the 70th time. An estimated 2,000,000 copies are in print

1973   Film version by Columbia Pictures Corporation, starring Peter Finch, Liv Ullmann and Michael York

1987   Publication of first sequel, *Return to Shangri-La* by Leslie Halliwell

1994   Publication of second sequel, *Messenger* by Frank De Marco

1996	Publication of third sequel, *Shangri-La,* by Eleanor Cooney, and Daniel Altieri
1996	William Morrow, New York, re-issues the novel in a facsimile of the first U.S. edition
1997	Reader's Digest Association publishes *Lost Horizon, Goodbye Mr. Chips* and *To You Mr. Chips* bound in one volume
2000	Centenary of Hilton's birth, formation of James Hilton Society to promote interest in his work
2003	Summersdale Publishers issue "70th Anniversary Edition" in Britain
2006	Pocket Books, New York, reprints the novel for the 105th time

Chapter Notes

Chapter 1

1. Hilton, *To You Mr. Chips* (London: Hodder & Stoughton, 1938), 12.
2. Ibid., 32–33.
3. Ibid., 33–34.
4. Hilton, *Goodbye Mr. Chips* (London: Hodder & Stoughton, 1934), 20.
5. Letter from Hilton, 24 November 1951, cited in Allan Foster, *The Movie Traveller* (Edinburgh: Polygon, 2000), 40.
6. Cited in *The Leys Fortnightly*, 13 July 1984, 14.
7. Hilton, *To You Mr. Chips*, 45.
8. Hilton, *Time and Time Again* (Boston: Little, Brown, 1953), 35.
9. Cited in Hilton, *Storm Passage* (London: Thornton Butterworth, 1922), 2.
10. Cited in Kausler, Introduction, in Hilton, *Storm Passage* (Shelburne, Canada: George Vanderburgh, 2003), 14.
11. Cited in "About the Author," in Hilton, *Lost Horizon* (Toronto: Macmillan Company of Canada, 1944), 237.
12. Hilton, *Terry* (London: Thornton Butterworth, 1927), 201.
13. Ibid., 90.
14. Hilton, *The Silver Flame* (London: Thornton Butterworth, 1928), 317–18.

15. Hilton, "Horizons Lost and Found," *The Stage*, February 1937, 42.
16. Ibid.
17. Cited on dust jacket of *Lost Horizon* (New York: William Morrow, 1996).
18. Ibid.
19. Preface, in Hilton, *Without Armor* (New York: Pocket Books, 1941), xi.
20. Letters from Hilton to Macmillan, 9 May 1933 and 11 May 1933, cited in Simon Nowell-Smith, ed., *Letters to Macmillan* (London: Macmillan, 1967), 345.
21. *Picturegoer*, 4 November 1939.
22. Ibid.; Preface, in Hilton, *Goodbye Mr. Chips* (Boston: Little Brown, 1935), vii.
23. Preface, in Hilton, *Goodbye Mr. Chips* (Boston: Little Brown, 1935), ix.
24. Cited in *Goodbye Mr. Chips* (London: Hodder Paperbacks, 1969), 3.
25. Hilton, *Entertainment World*, 7 November 1969. Cited in Michael Troyan, *A Rose for Mrs. Miniver* (Lexington: University Press of Kentucky, 1999), 89.
26. Cited in Christopher Silvester, ed., *The Penguin Book of Hollywood* (London: Penguin, 1998), 244.
27. "The Maligned Village," *Nash's Pall Mall Magazine*, April 1937, 78.

28. Cited in Kenneth Barrow, *Mr. Chips: The Life of Robert Donat* (London: Methuen, 1985), 111.

29. Cited in Leslie Halliwell, *Halliwell's Film Guide* (London: Paladin, 1989), 1097.

30. Hilton, *To You Mr. Chips* (London: Hodder & Stoughton, 1938), 55–56.

31. *New York Times Book Review*, 26 January 1941, p. 4.

32. Hilton, *Random Harvest* (London: Macmillan, 1941), 341.

33. *BBC Guide to Films* (London: BBC Worldwide, 2000), 1157.

34. Cited in Troyan, *A Rose for Mrs. Minever*, 125.

35. Cited in Halliwell, *Halliwell's Film Guide*, 687.

36. "Twilight of the Wise" (London: St. Hugh's, 1949); "Appassionata," *Good Housekeeping*, November-December 1941; "Shangri-La Is Where You Find It," *American Weekly*, 10 September 1955.

37. Hilton, *Nothing So Strange* (London: Macmillan, 1948), 295.

38. Cyril Clemens, "My Friend James Hilton" (*Hobbies*, July 1956), 109.

39. Hilton, *Lost Horizon* (New York: Pocket, 2005), 74, 141.

40. *The Times*, 22 December 1954.

41. Hilton, *To You Mr. Chips* (London: Hodder & Stoughton, 1938), 54.

Chapter 5

1. Hilton, Preface to Author's Edition of *Lost Horizon* (New York: William Morrow, 1936), vii–viii.

2. *Times Literary Supplement*, 28 September 1933, 648.

3. *Daily Telegraph*, 22 September 1933, 7.

4. *Everyman*, 6 October 1933, 26.

5. *Time and Tide*, 7 October 1933, 1186.

6. *Sphere*, 7 October 1933, 26.

7. *The Bookman*, December 1933, 1.

8. *New York Herald Tribune*, 15 October 1933.

9. *Saturday Review of Literature*, 14 October 1933, 181.

10. *Yale Review*, Winter 1934, vii.

11. *New York Times*, 15 October 1933.

12. *Canadian Forum*, December 1933, 112.

Chapter 6

1. Preface to the Author's Edition of *Lost Horizon* (New York: William Morrow, 1936), vii.

2. For a detailed account of the publishing history of Pan Books, see Richard Williams, *Pan Books 1945–1966: A Bibliographical Checklist* (Scunthorpe, U.K.: Dragonby, 1994).

Chapter 7

1. Hilton, Preface, *Without Armor* (New York: Pocket, 1941), x.

2. *Lockheed Vega Star*, 25 June 1943, 7.

3. Cited in Adrienne Reynolds, "Shangri-La," *James Hilton Newsletter*, January 2005, 9.

4. Hilton interviewed by Grant Uden, *The Bookman*, July 1934.

5. Hilton, radio broadcast, 10 September 1950. Cited in Adrienne Reynolds, "Shangri-La," *James Hilton Newsletter*, January 2005, 9.

6. Hilton interviewed by Grant Uden, *The Bookman*, July 1934.

7. Samuel H. Vasbinder, "Aspects of Fantasy in Literary Myths about Lost Civilizations," in *The Aesthetics of Fantasy Literature and Art*, edited by Roger C. Schlobin (Brighton, U.K.: Harvester, 1982), 196.

Chapter 8

1. Catalogue, Parke Bernet Galleries Inc., New York, "Rare First Editions Belonging to Frank Capra," April 1949.
2. Each of these writers was the author of at least one best-selling novel: Warwick Deeping, *Sorrel and Son* (1925), Howard Spring, *My Son, My Son* (1938), Arthur Hutchinson, *If Winter Comes* (1921) and Michael Arlen, *The Green Hat* (1924).
3. *Daily Telegraph,* 22 September 1933, 7.
4. Letter to the author from an English-speaking reading group at Monaco.
5. Compare also Howat Freemantle in *And Now Goodbye* and A.J. Fothergill in *Without Armor.*
6. James W. Poling, *New York Herald Tribune,* 15 October 1933.
7. Francis S Heck, "The Domain as a Symbol of a Paradise Lost," *Nassau Review,* Vol. 4, No. 3 (1982): 29.
8. "A Gossip on Romance," *Longman's Magazine,* November 1882. Reprinted as Chapter 15 of *Memories and Portraits.*
9. Susan Hill, "Come You Back to Manderley," *Daily Telegraph,* circa 1976.

Chapter 9

1. Jeremy Hawthorn, *Unlocking the Text* (London: Arnold, 1987), 43, 51.
2. George Dangerfield, "James Hilton's Fantasy," *Saturday Review of Literature,* Vol. 14 (October 1933): 181.
3. William Kenney, *James Hilton's Lost Horizon* (New York: Monarch, 1966), 58.
4. Joseph Campbell, *The Hero with a Thousand Faces* (London: Paladin, 1988), 97.
5. Leo Marx, *The Machine in the Garden* (New York: Oxford University Press, 1964), 229.

6. Hilton, *Random Harvest* (London: Macmillan, 1941), 179.
7. Kenney, *James Hilton's Lost Horizon,* 9.
8. Peter Bishop, *The Myth of Shangri-La* (London: Athlone, 1989), 216.
9. Interview with Grant Uden, *The Bookman,* July 1934.
10. H.G. Wells, *An Englishman Looks at the World* (London: Cassell, 1914), 204.
11. Hilton, "A Chapter of Autobiography," in *To You Mr. Chips* (London: Hodder & Stoughton, 1938), 15.

Chapter 10

1. Lawrence J. Quirk, *The Great Romantic Films* (Secaucus, NJ: Citadel, 1974), 53; R. Dixon Smith, *Ronald Colman, Gentleman of the Cinema* (Jefferson, NC: McFarland, 1991), 175; Juliet Benita Colman, *Ronald Colman* (London: W.H. Allen, 1975), 174.
2. Cited in Leslie Halliwell, *Halliwell's Film Guide* (London: Paladin, 1989), 616.
3. Cited in Colman, *Ronald Colman,* 175.
4. "The Maligned Village," *Nash's Pall Mall Magazine,* April 1937, 74–78.
5. Leslie Halliwell, *Halliwell's Hundred* (London: Paladin, 1982), 182.
6. "The Maligned Village."
7. Smith, *Ronald Colman,* 188.
8. Leonard Maltin, *Movie and Video Guide* (New York: Penguin, 2002), 829; *Radio Times Guide to Films* (London: BBC Worldwide, 2000), 852; Halliwell, *Halliwell's Film Guide,* 616; Quirk, *The Great Romantic Films,* 55.
9. "The Maligned Village."
10. I am indebted to Dr. Sally Plowright of the Royal College of Music, London, for much of this information. The details are taken from S. Plowright, "Harry Warren and His Contribution to Twentieth Century

American Popular Song and the Film Musical" (Ph.D. thesis), 286–88.

Chapter 11

1. Harold Martin, "The Road to Shangri-La," in *Lost Horizon,* School Edition (New York: William Morrow, 1962), xi.
2. Ibid., xii.
3. John W Crawford, "Utopian Eden of *Lost Horizon,*" *Extrapolation,* Vol. 22, No. 2 (1981): 190.
4. John Fowles, Afterword, in Alain-Fournier, *The Lost Domain* (Oxford: Oxford University Press, 1986), 286–87.
5. James Gunn, ed., *The New Encyclopaedia of Science Fiction* (New York: Viking Penguin, 1988), 225.
6. Brian Stableford, "Yesterday's Bestsellers: *Lost Horizon.*" *Million,* January 1993, 46.
7. John Clute and John Grant, eds., *The Encyclopaedia of Fantasy* (London: Orbit, 1977), 468.
8. Paul Simpson, Michaela Bushell and Helen Rodiss, eds., *The Rough Guide to Cult Fiction* (London: Penguin, 2005), 292–93.
9. Eleanor Cooney and Daniel Altieri, *Shangri-La* (New York: William Morrow, 1996), 232.
10. Ibid., 253.

11. Timothy Carroll, "Could This Be the Way to Shangri-La?" *Daily Telegraph,* 29 July 2002, 3.
12. Peter Bishop, *The Myth of Shangri-La* (London: Athlone, 1989), 211.
13. Martin Brauen, *Dreamworld Tibet* (Bangkok, Thailand: Orchid, 2004), 85.
14. Abebooks website, www.abebooks.com, accessed 11 August 2002.
15. Coles Notes on *Lost Horizon* (London: Coles, 1965) 6.
16. William Kenney, "James Hilton's *Lost Horizon"* (New York: Monarch, 1966), 58.
17. *Dictionary of National Biography* (Oxford: Oxford University Press, 2004).
18. *Time,* 18 November 1935, p. 30.
19. A.C. Ward, *Longman Companion to Twentieth Century Literature* (London: Longman, 1975), 257.
20. Kenney, "James Hilton's *Lost Horizon,*" 5.
21. Richard Church, *British Authors: A Twentieth Century Gallery* (London: Longman, 1943), 136.
22. Cited in Nina Bowden, Preface, *Someone at a Distance* (London: Persephone Books, 1994), vi.
23. Jeremy Hawthorn, *Unlocking the Text* (London: Edward Arnold, 1987), 6.
24. *Waltham Forest News,* 17 July 1997, 8.
25. Wells, Introduction, *The Country of the Blind and Other Stories* (London: Nelson, 1911), ix.

Bibliography of Secondary Works

Books

Baker, Ian. *The Heart of the World: A Journey to the Last Secret Place.* New York: Penguin Press, 2005.

Barrow, Kenneth. *Mr. Chips: The Life of Robert Donat.* London: Methuen, 1985.

Bell, Michael, ed. *The Context of English Literature 1900–1930.* London: Methuen, 1980.

Bishop, Peter. *The Myth of Shangri-La.* London: Athlone, 1989.

Bloom, Clive. *Bestsellers: Popular Fiction since 1900.* London: Palgrave, 2002.

Bradbury, Malcolm. *The Social Context of Modern English Literature.* Oxford: Basil Blackwell, 1971.

_____. *What Is a Novel?* London: Edward Arnold, 1969.

Brauen, Martin. *Dreamworld Tibet.* Bangkok, Thailand: Orchid, 2004.

Campbell, Joseph. *The Hero with a Thousand Faces.* London: Paladin, 1988.

Chetwynd, Tom. *A Dictionary of Symbols.* London: Paladin, 1982.

Church, Richard. *British Authors: A Twentieth Century Gallery.* London: Longmans, 1948.

Cirlot, J.E. *A Dictionary of Symbols.* London: Routledge, 1962.

Clute, John, and John Grant, eds. *The Encyclopaedia of Fantasy.* London: Orbit, 1997.

Clute, John, and Peter Nicholls, eds. *The Encyclopaedia of Science Fiction.* London: Orbit, 1993.

Colman, Juliet Benita. *Ronald Colman: A Very Private Person.* London: W.H. Allen, 1975.

Columbia Pictures Corporation. *The Making of a Great Picture.* 1937.

Bibliography of Secondary Works

Cooney, Eleanor, and Daniel Altieri. *Shangri-La*. New York: William Morrow, 1996.

Daiches, David. *Critical Approaches to Literature*, Second Edition. London: Longman, 1981.

De Marco, Frank *Messenger: A Sequel to Lost Horizon*. Norfolk, VA: Hampton Roads, 1994.

Elliott, Robert C. *The Shape of Utopia*. Chicago: University of Chicago Press, 1970.

Foster, Allen. *The Movie Traveller*. Edinburgh: PolyGram, 2000.

Gunn, James, ed. *The New England Encyclopaedia of Science Fiction*. New York: Viking Penguin, 1988.

Halliwell, Leslie. *The Filmgoer's Companion*. London: Macgibbon and Kee, 1967.

_____. *Halliwell's Film Guide*. Seventh Edition. London: Paladin, 1989.

_____. *Halliwell's Hundred*. London: Paladin, 1982.

_____. *Return to Shangri La*. London: Grafton, 1987.

_____. *Seats in All Parts*. London: Grafton, 1986.

Hammond, John R. *H.G. Wells's The Time Machine: A Reference Guide*. Westport, CT: Praeger, 2004.

Harrer, Heinrich. *Seven Years in Tibet*. London: Hart-Davis, 1953.

Hawthorn, Jeremy. *Studying the Novel*. London: Edward Arnold, 1985.

_____. *Unlocking the Text*. London: Edward Arnold, 1987.

Hayes, Dale Garfan. *Hilton's Lost Horizon*. Lincoln, NE: Cliffs, 1980.

Hutchinson, Peter. *Games Authors Play*. London: Methuen, 1983.

Jackson, Rosemary. *Fantasy: The Literature of Subversion*. London: Methuen, 1981.

Johnson, Robert A. *The Psychology of Romantic Love*. London: Arkana, 1983.

Kenney, William. *James Hilton's Lost Horizon*. New York: Monarch, 1966.

Lodge, David. *Language of Fiction*. London: Routledge, 1966.

MacQueen, John. *Allegory*. London: Methuen, 1970.

Maltin, Leonard. *Movie and Video Guide*. New York: Penguin, 2002.

Manguel, Alberto, and Gianni Guadalupi. *The Dictionary of Imaginary Places*. London: Bloomsbury, 1999.

Marx, Leo. *The Machine in the Garden: Technology and the Pastoral Ideal*. New York: Oxford University Press, 1964.

McFarlane, Brian. *Novel to Film*. Oxford: Clarendon, 1996.

McGilligan, Pat, ed. *Six Screenplays by Robert Riskin*. Berkeley, CA: University of California Press, 1997.

McRae, Michael. *In Search of Shangri La*. London: Michael Joseph, 2004.

Morgan, Charles. *The House of Macmillan 1843–1943*. London: Macmillan, 1943.

Nowell-Smith, Simon, ed. *Letters to Macmillan*. London: Macmillan, 1967.

Ondaatje, Michael, ed. *Lost Classics*. London: Bloomsbury, 2003.

Poague, Leland. *Another Frank Capra*. Cambridge: Cambridge University Press, 1994.

Quinlan, David. *Quinlan's Film Stars*. London: Batsford, 1981.

Quirk, Lawrence J. *The Great Romantic Films*. Secausus, NJ: Citadel, 1974.

Righter, William. *Myth and Literature*. London: Routledge and Kegan Paul, 1975.

Rohmann, Chris. *The Dictionary of Important Ideas and Thinkers.* London: Hutchinson, 2000.

Schlobin, Roger C., ed. *The Aesthetics of Fantasy Literature and Art.* Brighton, U.K.: Harvester Press, 1982.

Seymour-Smith, Martin. *Novels and Novelists.* London: Windward, 1980.

Silvester, Christopher, ed. *The Penguin Book of Hollywood.* London: Penguin, 1998.

Simpson, Paul, Michaela Bushell, and Helen Radiss, eds. *The Rough Guide to Cult Fiction.* London: Penguin, 2005.

Smith, R. Dixon. *Ronald Colman: Gentleman of the Cinema.* Jefferson, NC: McFarland, 1991.

Snodgrass, Mary Ellen. *Encyclopaedia of Utopian Literature.* Santa Barbara, CA: ABC-Clio, 1995.

Stableford, Brian. *Yesterday's Best Sellers.* London: Borgo, 1998.

Symons, Julian. *The Angry Thirties.* London: Eyre Methuen, 1976.

Thomas, Lowell. *Out of This World: Across the Himalayas to Tibet.* London: Macdonald, 1951.

Troyan, Michael. *A Rose for Mrs. Miniver: The Life of Greer Garson.* Lexington: University Press of Kentucky, 1999.

Walsh, Chad. *From Utopia to Nightmare.* London: Geoffrey Bles, 1962.

Watts, Stephen. *Stars and Films of 1937.* London: Daily Express Publications, 1937.

Weston, Jessie L. *From Ritual to Romance.* New York: Doubleday, 1957.

Articles

Baker, Ian. "Paradise Found." *Independent on Sunday,* 6 March 2005, pp. 27–31.

Buckley, Michael. "In Search of Shangri-La." *Nuvo,* Autumn 2004, pp. 104–108.

Callan, Paul. "Did This Man Know Where Shangri-La Really Was?" *Daily Express,* 11 March 2000, pp. 34–35.

Carroll, Timothy. "Could This Be the Way to Shangri-La?" *Daily Telegraph,* 29 July 2002, p. 3.

Clemens, Cyril. "My Friend James Hilton." *Hobbies,* July 1956, pp. 106–109.

Crawford, John W. "Utopian Eden of Lost Horizon." *Extrapolation,* Vol. 22, No. 2 (1981): 186–190.

Cunningham, James P. "Lost Horizon." *The Commonweal,* March 26, 1937, p. 612.

Hammond, John R. "A Centenary Tribute to James Hilton." *This England,* Autumn 2000, pp. 50–51.

_____. "Collecting Hilton in Paperback." *James Hilton Newsletter,* October 2005, pp. 5–6.

_____. "In Search of Shangri-La." *Slightly Foxed,* Spring 2006, pp. 82–85.

Heck, Francis S. "The Domain as a Symbol of a Paradise Lost: *Lost Horizon* and *Brideshead Revisited?" Nassau Review,* Vol. 4, No. 3 (1982): 24–29.

Bibliography of Secondary Works

Hilton, James. "Ceiling Unlimited." Series of six radio broadcasts on the Columbia Broadcasting System. Lockheed Aircraft Corporation, 1943.
_____. "Challenge of Mount Everest." *Esquire*, July 1948, pp. 58, 146.
_____. "A Chapter of Autobiography." *To You Mr. Chips*. London: Hodder & Stoughton, 1938, pp. 11–63.
_____._____. "Horizons Lost and Found." *The Stage*, February 1937, p. 42.
Liu, Melinda. "Searching for Shangri-La." *Newsweek*, 26 March 2001, pp. 45–47.
Martin, Harold C. "The Road to Shangri-La." *Lost Horizon*, School Edition. New York: William Morrow, 1962, pp. vii–xiii.
Stableford, Brian. "Yesterday's Bestsellers: *Lost Horizon*." *Million*, January 1993, pp. 43–46.

Bibliography of Hilton's Works

Fiction

Catherine Herself. London: Unwin, 1920.

Storm Passage. London: Unwin, 1922.

The Passionate Year. London: Butterworth, 1923; Boston: Little, Brown, 1924.

The Dawn of Reckoning. London: Butterworth, 1925; New York: King, 1932 [U.S. Title: *Rage in Heaven*].

The Meadows of the Moon. London: Butterworth, 1926; Boston: Small, Maynard, 1927.

Terry. London: Butterworth, 1927.

The Silver Flame. London: Butterworth, 1928; New York: Avon, 1949 [U.S. Title: *Three Loves Had Margaret*].

And Now Goodbye. London: Benn, 1931; New York: Morrow, 1932.

Murder at School. London: Benn, 1931; New York: Harper, 1933 [also published under the title *Was It Murder?*].

Contango. London: Benn, 1932; New York: Morrow, 1932 [U.S. Title: *Ill Wind*].

Lost Horizon. London: Macmillan, 1933; New York: Morrow, 1933.

Knight without Armour. London: Benn, 1933; New York: Morrow, 1934 [U.S. Title: *Without Armour*].

Goodbye Mr. Chips. London: Hoddder & Stoughton, 1924; Boston: Little Brown, 1934.

We Are Not Alone. London: Macmillan, 1937; Boston: Little Brown, 1937.

Goodbye Mr. Chips: A Play in Three Acts [with Barbara Burnham]. London: Hodder & Stoughton, 1938.

To You Mr. Chips. London: Hodder & Stoughton, 1938.

Random Harvest. London: Macmillan, 1941; Boston: Little Brown, 1941.

So Well Remembered. Boston: Little Brown, 1945; London: Macmillan, 1947.
Nothing So Strange. Boston: Little Brown, 1947; London: Macmillan, 1948.
Morning Journey. London: Macmillan, 1951; Boston: Little Brown, 1951.
Time and Time Again. London: Macmillan, 1953; Boston: Little Brown, 1953.

Nonfiction

Mr. Chips Looks at the World. Los Angeles: Modern Forum, 1939.
The Story of Dr. Wassell. Boston: Little Brown, 1943; London: Macmillan, 1944.
H.R.H.: The Story of Philip, Duke of Edinburgh. Boston: Little Brown, 1956; London: Muller, 1956 [published posthumously].

Index

Index

title 122
To You Mr Chips 27
Tolkien, J.R.R. 122, 168
"Twilight of the Wise" 32

utopia 131–135

Vaill, Edward 164–165

Wall Street crash 54, 86
Walthamstow 5, 6
Ward, A.C. 171

Warner, H.B. 142
We Are Not Alone 27
Wells, H.G. 9, 37, 85, 99, 113, 116, 125, 156
West, Claudine 30, 190
Wimperis, Arthur 30, 190
Without Armor see *Knight Without Armour*
Woodford Green 10, 11, 174
Woollcott, Alexander 190
Wright, S. Fowler 125, 157
Wyatt, Jane 142, 164

Younghusband, Francis 91

DATE DUE

DEMCO 25-380